MEND & PATCH

MEND & PATCH

A HANDBOOK TO REPAIRING CLOTHES AND TEXTILES

KERSTIN NEUMÜLLER

PAVILION

Foreword

Surely, one of the saddest things ever is to throw a beloved favourite garment away because it's got holes in it? Over the years I've met many people who have had their own solutions to the problem, and what fascinates me is that there aren't any rights or wrongs. After spending a week with a mender who made miraculously invisible repairs by weaving in a piece of fabric over the hole, I met up with my punk mate who said, 'Yes, of course – I always carry my mending kit with me!' And then he fished textile glue and a patch with a band name printed on it out of his bag. Whenever his trousers tore – and it happened quite often – he would simply glue on a new patch and that was that!

Today I run a clothes store in Stockholm together with my partner Douglas, who is a material nerd just like me. We fill our shop with garments that are made to last and that just get better with time. But even the best clothes will tear sooner or later, so in the furthest corner of the shop we've set up a mending studio. When it's quiet in the shop, I sit there by the sewing machine and give a new lease of life to people's favourite old jeans. Some people prefer discreet and invisible repairs, while others want them to take pride of place and be highly visible. I think that the care you show when mending a garment strengthens your connection to it, as if the repair becomes a part of the history of the person who wears the garment. Many jeans come back to the mending studio year after year and, in a way, you can follow the wearers' lives by looking at their jeans! Wear from tobacco boxes and phones appears or disappears, someone starts to cycle and wears down the right leg on the chain, someone else has a baby and the jeans tear on the knees from spending so much time on the floor.

It might seem as if I want to pick on those who like to buy new clothes – but it's actually the other way around! Buy what you want, and try to find the most hardwearing and durable variety. When your favourite garments have had their wear and tear, take out this book and save them.

Kerstin Neumüller

Before you start

For those who don't sleep with a needle and thread under their pillow, mending a garment might feel like a big undertaking – but do it in small steps and it will be fine. My first and best tip is to work with fabrics that you like, because it's a lot more fun to mend with a patch of a nice fabric than with something you've found at the bottom of the sock drawer.

All damaged garments can be mended, but sometimes it can involve replacing the majority of the fabric surface – and in these cases you have to ask yourself whether it's worth the work. If it's the first time you've done any mending, it's a good idea to make a little test patch before you start to get a feel for the technique.

WHAT DOES GOOD QUALITY ACTUALLY MEAN?

Good-quality garments will last for longer before they tear, and they are also often easier to mend than garments that are produced with the primary aim being to make them cheap. The tricky thing with the term 'quality' is that there are many interpretations of what the word actually means; it's very often used to describe something that is generally good, so the word's meaning has started to become diluted.

When it comes to clothes, I usually look out for natural materials that aren't mixed with synthetics. It's not that clothes from synthetic materials can't be of good quality, but the mix usually isn't that great. I also tend to look at the garment's seams to see if any threads are loose and, most importantly, I feel the fabric to check if it's something I would like to wear against my body.

I completely avoid clothes that have been treated to look as if they've already been worn for a long time – for example, jeans that have been washed multiple times, and sometimes also ripped in various artful ways, to make them look as if they've already been worn for a few years before they reached the shop shelf. This all has an effect on the quality and these clothes tend to have a much shorter lifespan than clothes without artificial wear and tear.

9

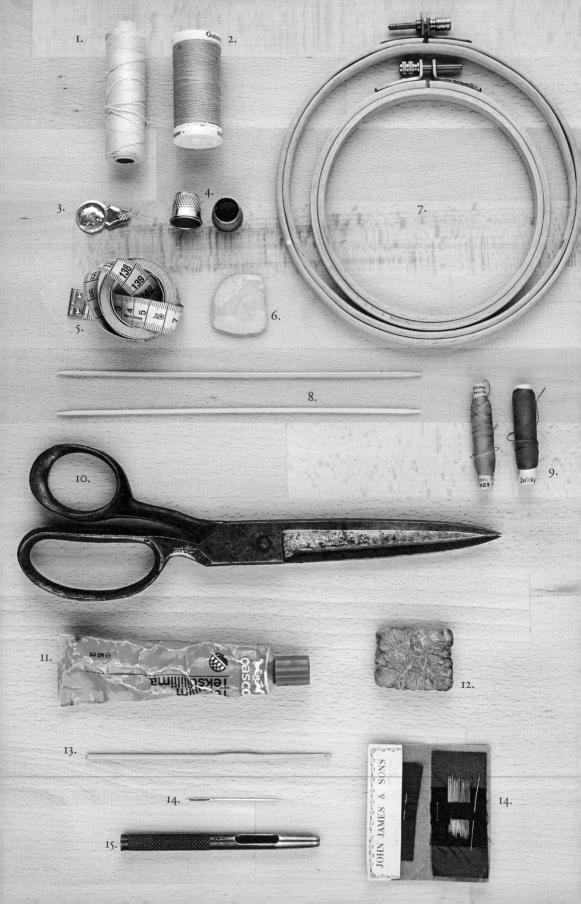

ESSENTIAL EQUIPMENT

1. LINEN THREAD – Linen thread isn't essential, but it's very pretty to sew with. Shiny and strong!

2. SEWING MACHINE THREAD – My mum says that Gütermann threads are the best and I've never had any reason to doubt that.

3. NEEDLE THREADER – Slot the little wire loop through the eye of the needle and insert the thread into the loop. Pull through both the loop and the thread, and the needle is threaded without you having to pinpoint its eye!

4. OPEN-ENDED THIMBLE – Similar to a standard thimble. Put one on the finger you use for pushing the needle through the fabric when sewing by hand to avoid getting pockmarked dents in your fingers.

5. TAPE MEASURE – For measuring things. More flexible than a ruler.

6. TAILOR'S CHALK – Can be bought in haberdashery shops and is used for marking where to put your stitches. In emergencies, blackboard chalks can be used as a substitute.

7. EMBROIDERY HOOP – Used for stretching a fabric that you want to hand sew and to prevent the fabric from puckering while you work on it. Release the screw to separate the two hoops and place one hoop on either side of the fabric that you want to stretch. Push the smaller hoop into the larger one, so that the fabric in between is taut and flat, and then tighten the screw again.

8. KNITTING NEEDLES – I usually use double-pointed needles.

9. SILK THREAD – Buy at flea markets. Sort them by colour or just chuck them into a tin. Useful for many decorative and strong seams.

10. SCISSORS – Get a sharp pair of scissors if you're intending to cut a lot of fabric!

11. TEXTILE GLUE – You can get both water-based and latex-based textile glue. I prefer latex-based, because it's the quickest to dry.

12. BEESWAX – Used for waxing threads for hand sewing.

13. CROCHET HOOK – Perfect for picking up unravelled stitches on knitted garments.

14. NEEDLES – Invest in a few different sizes. A needle that's too thick can be impossible to use for sewing dense fabrics and is more suitable for loosely woven fabrics, while a needle that is too thin will bend and break if you use it for sewing thick fabrics.

15. HOLLOW PUNCH – A metal rod with a circular die in one end that can be used for punching round holes in things.

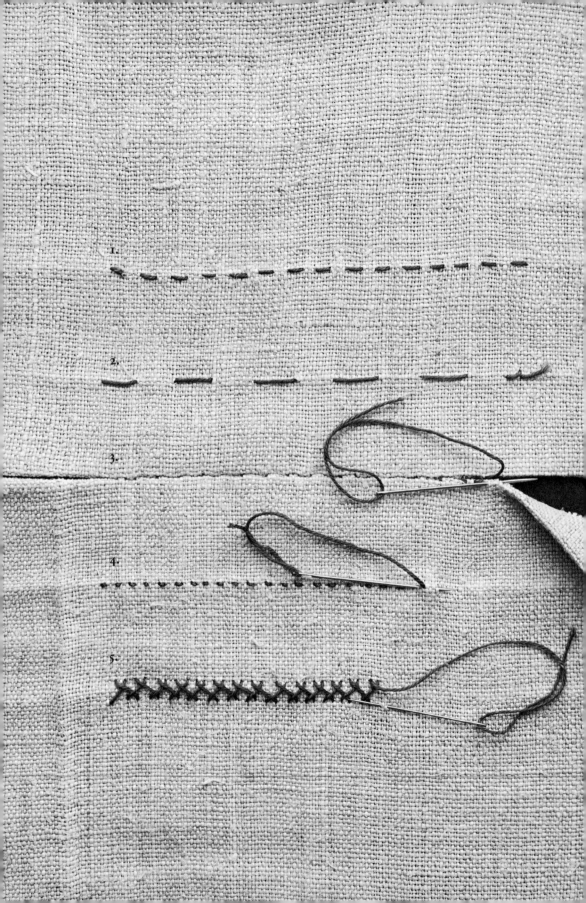

STITCHES

1. RUNNING STITCH
I usually call it 'standard up-and-down stitch' if people think 'running stitch' sounds strange.

2. TACKING (BASTING) STITCH
Used instead of pins to hold layers of fabric in place while sewing. You can tack using a long running stitch or do rough diagonal stitches.

3. SLIPSTITCH
Similar to a running stitch, this is sewn through two pieces of fabric to keep them together. Perfect for when a seam has split!

4. PICK STITCH
Almost like a running stitch, but the needle is inserted just behind the place where it came out. The result is a stitch that is very visible from the wrong side of the fabric, but not very visible on the right side.

5. CATCH STITCH
A stitch that is good for keeping fabric edges in place and at the same time shows very little on the right side of the garment. When you insert the needle into the fabric, you pick up as few threads as possible (one or two are usually enough) and the seam can be virtually invisible.

6. STRAIGHT STITCH

The most common machine stitch, this is used for joining together pieces of fabric. Secure by reversing a few stitches and then going a few steps forwards at the beginning and end of the seam.

7. ZIGZAG STITCH

The second most common stitch on a sewing machine. Used for preventing fabric edges from fraying and for sewing stretchy seams. It is secured in the same way as straight stitch.

8. BLIND HEM STITCH

Used to join one fabric edge to another.

9. SECURING A THREAD BY REVERSE STITCHING

If you want to avoid knots when starting or finishing a seam, insert the needle from the wrong side of the fabric about 1 cm (½ in.) beyond the point at which the seam would start, and sew backwards for a couple of stitches before you start sewing the seam. The thread will be secured through friction. This method of securing the thread is good when you are working with thicker threads, but it is not suitable for sewing machine thread.

10. SECURING A THREAD WITH A KNOT

Tie a knot on the thread you are sewing with and insert the needle from the wrong side of the fabric at the seam's starting point. When it's time to secure the thread, sew a knot by sewing a little stitch in the fabric and then inserting the needle through the loop that has formed. Repeat one more time in the same place and then cut off the thread.

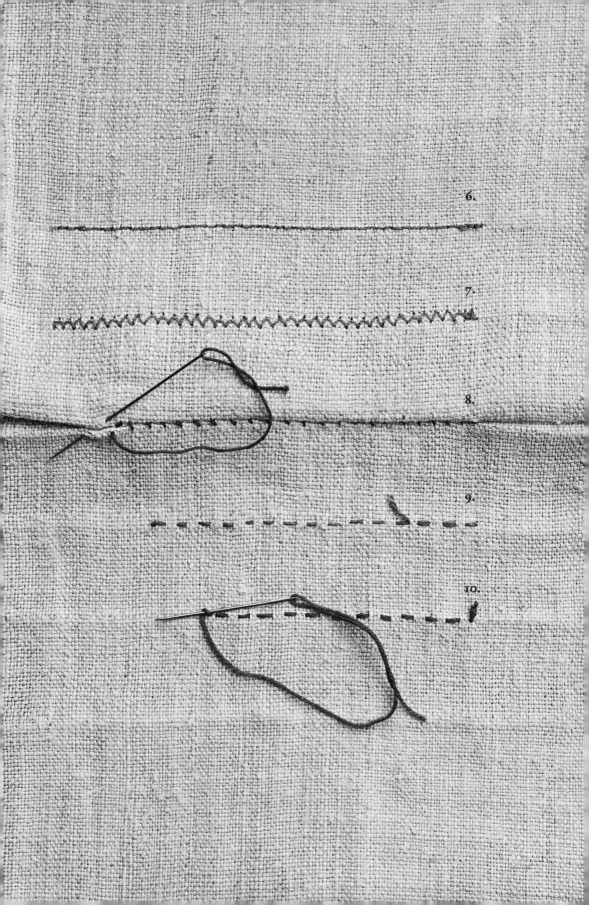

6.

7.

8.

9.

10.

WHAT'S THE DAMAGE?

Before you start planning the design of your mend, it's good to identify what the damage is. There are many types of holes and most are due to a tear in the fabric, but sometimes it's just a seam that has ripped and that's quick to mend. Take a closer look at the hole and you'll be able to see what's wrong.

There are two main causes of holes appearing in fabric. The first is that the fabric has worn down; this is often the case with the elbows and knees of garments that have been used a lot. In this situation, it's not enough to just mend the actual hole, since the surrounding fabric will also have worn thin and will be in need of reinforcement. The other cause of holes is more direct. Tears and holes can be caused from encounters with thorny bushes or moths and appear on fabrics that are otherwise relatively new and strong; here, you can focus on just mending the actual hole.

If the garment is too tight for the wearer, a sneaky kind of hole can appear – the fabric will start to fray just next to the seam. This is particularly common with the back seams on waistcoats and under the arms on shirts. The problem can often be rectified by unpicking the seam, mending the fabric and then sewing the seam back together again with a slightly smaller seam allowance than the original. This way the garment becomes a bit more spacious!

TACKING (BASTING)

Tacking can be used in place of pins to hold several layers of fabric together, or to mark a guide line for sewing, instead of chalk. Tacking is always temporary and is removed once the sewing project has been completed. There is a special tacking thread made from cotton that is thicker and more loosely spun than standard sewing thread to make it easier to remove when it's no longer needed, but you can also use standard sewing thread for tacking.

Tacking might seem like a boring job but I've learned from experience that it's worth the effort, since it will then be easier to work on the mending – plus the end result will look neater. You might think, 'I don't need to do this' – but that's not true. Get tacking!

When tacking, you will usually use running stitch. It doesn't matter in the least what it looks like, as long as it holds all the bits in place, because you'll remove the tacking thread once you've sewn the actual seam.

CHOOSING THREAD

A carefully chosen thread can really lift the whole mend; in the same way, the wrong thread can mean that the mend ends up looking not very nice at all and, in the worst cases, is not even functional. The material the thread is made from will determine its qualities, so it's a good idea to carefully consider it before you start sewing. For hand sewing I usually use thread made from cotton or linen, which results in soft and supple repairs. If you want the stitches to be clearly visible, it's good to use a thick thread. I often look through thin knitting, crochet and weaving yarns to find threads that feel right.

When sewing on a machine I usually use polyester thread, especially when mending jeans. This is because polyester thread is more durable than cotton thread, so it's useful when you're mending garments that are subjected to a lot of wear and tear. On the other hand, a cotton thread will blend into a cotton fabric better. It simply comes down to personal preference.

If you want your mending to be as invisible as possible, it's good to take a bit of extra time over choosing your thread. It's easy to think that a blue thread will blend into a blue fabric, but you can rarely chance it, so bring the garment that you are mending to the shop and pick out a thread colour that is as close to the colour of the garment as possible. It's a good idea to choose a thread that looks slightly greyer than the garment, as this will blend in better with the fabric that is to be mended.

LENGTH OF THREAD

When sewing by hand it's tempting to use a thread that is as long as possible to avoid having to fasten off the thread too often. Unfortunately, it's the exact opposite of practical – as you will notice after only a few stitches, when the thread gets caught and starts to form knots. A good length of thread for sewing by hand is about an arm's length.

SECURING THE THREAD

There are several ways to secure a thread. When sewing by machine, it's common to sew a few stitches forwards, then reverse for a few stitches and then start sewing the seam. At the end of the seam secure the thread in the same way, by reversing for a few stitches.

When sewing by hand, you can secure the thread at the start of a seam by tying a knot at the end of the thread and inserting the needle from the wrong side of the project. At the end of the seam or when the thread is almost used up, take the needle through to the wrong side of the fabric and sew a little knot around the previous stitch.

In hand sewing, you can also secure a thread by reverse stitching. This method is most suitable for slightly thicker threads, where a knot would be more obvious. Insert the needle about 1 cm (½ in.) ahead of where you want to start the seam and then sew backwards for a few stitches until you reach the seam's starting point. Then turn and sew back through your own stitches in order to lock the thread in place without having to create a knot on either side. When the thread is coming to an end, turn the work and sew a few stitches to cover those you have already sewn in order to secure the thread.

MENDING LINED GARMENTS

When you're mending the outer fabric of a lined garment, it's often best to unpick a seam in the lining so that you can reach the area you need to get at without risking sewing into the lining – but there are exceptions. When doing smaller repairs by hand, it's usually enough to loosen the lining just a little.

Unpick enough of the seam of the lining to insert a piece of paper about 1 cm (½ in.) larger than the hole you are mending, slotting it in between the lining and the outer fabric. Now secure the piece of paper in place using pins, or even better, by tacking (basting) it in place and then start your mending. The paper will work like a protective layer in between the two fabrics while at the same time keeping the outer fabric stretched.

PRESSING

In both ironing and pressing, you use a hot iron to straighten out the fabric, but that's where the similarities end. Ironing involves moving the iron in wide motions over the fabric to straighten it out, but when you press you keep the iron still in one place for a few seconds.

Ironing is used to take the creases out of fabrics after washing. Pressing is used to give shape to a garment or for flattening details in newly sewn or, in this case, newly mended garments.

When pressing you almost always use a damp cloth, known as a pressing cloth, between the iron and the fabric. You can make a good pressing cloth yourself from two 25-cm (10-in.) square pieces of cotton fabric (an old bedsheet, for example) that you zigzag together along the edges, so that the finished cloth is made up of a double layer of fabric. The pressing cloth will protect the fabric from the heat from the iron, which can otherwise leave shiny marks on the fabric; at the same time, steam is produced when the damp cloth is heated up by the hot iron.

HOW TO PRESS

Set the iron to a warm temperature and place the part of the garment that you want to press on the ironing board. Wet the pressing cloth and wring it out. Straighten out the cloth and place it over the part of the fabric that you want to press. Place the iron on top of the cloth and press down for approximately 4–6 seconds. The cloth will hiss, but that's okay.

Lift the iron, remove the cloth and let the steam evaporate a little. If you want, you can press again using the part of the pressing cloth that is now dry. Leave the fabric to cool a little before you remove it from the ironing board.

THIMBLES

When you sew by hand, you may notice after a while that your fingers hurt a bit. Pushing the needle through the fabric and pulling it out on the other side can cause sore fingertips that don't exactly encourage you to continue with your project. I've tried many tricks in order to avoid this – everything from sticking plasters to taping small coins to my fingertips – but the real game-changer came when I learned how to use a thimble. Since then, my fingers have pulled through relatively unscathed.

A thimble is like a little metal hat for your finger. An open-ended thimble is similar, but without a 'roof', allowing the fingertip to protrude a little. I use both in the same way, and it doesn't really matter which model you choose: the main thing is that the thimble can sit on your right hand's middle finger (if you're right-handed) without feeling uncomfortable and without falling off. You hold the needle between your index finger and thumb, and you use the inside of your armoured middle finger to push the needle through the fabric.

It can feel a bit awkward to start with, but it's worth persevering because you'll soon sew quicker – and without any bloodshed!

COMMON MISTAKES

Think of this list of common errors as someone else making the mistakes for you, so that you don't have to!

PATCHES TOO THICK – Very common, especially when mending jeans. Go ahead and mend with a denim fabric if you want to – but use one that is thin, otherwise the mend will often feel like a hard cake.

ONLY PATCHING THE HOLE AND NOT THE WORN SURROUNDING FABRIC – Look at the fabric around the hole: what does it look like? Is it on the brink of tearing as well? Sometimes it can be easy to spot fragile areas if you hold the fabric up against a light source or turn the fabric inside out. Cut out the worst part and reinforce the rest, otherwise the fabric next to the hole will soon tear as well.

SEWING TOGETHER A TEAR – If you place two edges of a hole next to each other and stitch them together, you actually remove even more fabric, and the garment will most likely tear again just next to the seam.

SEWING DOWN THE POCKET ON THE INSIDE OF A GARMENT – You have managed to squeeze a pair of jeans onto the sewing machine and started to mend the crotch, but before long you notice that the pocket has been sewn down, too. It takes ages to unpick. Avoid this by always checking that the pocket hasn't managed to sneak in before you start sewing.

TOO MUCH GLUE – If you're using glue, you should only use a tiny amount to keep the repair in place until you have sewn it together. Too much glue will create a hard cake and leave ugly stains, and it will also lose strength over time so that the patch comes off again. The glue, on the other hand, will never come off!

PULLING THE THREAD TOO TIGHT – You won't get a stronger repair by pulling the thread really tight when you sew by hand; instead, you'll end up with a bulky, puckered repair. Pull the stitch tight enough for it not to sit like a loop on the fabric's surface, but not so tight so that it cuts into the fabric like an angry line. It should feel like a happy little grain of rice!

NOT MENDING IN TIME – The saying 'a stitch in time saves nine' is actually true. Mend as soon as you discover the damage and it will be so much easier to repair than if you leave it for another few weeks. I can't say that I always keep to this rule myself, but I wish I did.

WRONG CHOICE OF THREAD – If you use a standard sewing thread for a hand-sewn repair that you want to be visible, there's a chance that you will be disappointed, since the stitches will be small and difficult to see. Choose a thicker thread for a better result.

WHEN YOU'RE IN A HURRY

Sometimes it's just not possible to sit down for several hours and sew an artistically accomplished repair; it's often just as you're about to leave home that you discover that the garment you were intending to wear has got a hole in it. Here are a few tips for when you want to wear a particular garment immediately but have just realized that it's damaged.

SEWING A BUTTON ONTO A GARMENT WITHOUT A LINING

Unfortunately, the buttons in most of the clothes that we buy today are poorly secured in all respects. This is because there are special sewing machines that are used solely for sewing on buttons, but they're usually not that good at securing the threads at the end. It can be tempting to pull the little thread that protrudes from the button — and if you've ever done it you probably know that it often leads to pulling the whole thread off, resulting in the button coming off. But keep calm: sewing on a button is quick and it's actually really simple. The trick is to create a tiny space in between the button and the fabric, since that's where the fabric that is buttoned needs to fit into. This small space is called the shank, and tailors do it by positioning the button a little bit away from the fabric when sewing it on. If it feels awkward, you can use a standard table fork to create the gap.

YOU WILL NEED: *Thread to match the button, it doesn't have to be a specialist thread; you can use standard sewing thread. Needle. Fork.*

Start by securing the thread with a knot on the wrong side of the fabric. Insert the needle where you want the button to sit and grab hold of a fork. Holding the fork in place in between the button and the fabric, sew the button on. You will need to make several stitches to ensure the button is properly secured. Once it feels like it's secured, make a few extra stitches; around 8–10 is good. Then pull out the fork and wrap the thread you've used to sew with a few times around the shank so that all the threads you've used to sew the button on are pulled together. Secure the thread by sewing a few stitches through the button's shank and then cut off the thread.

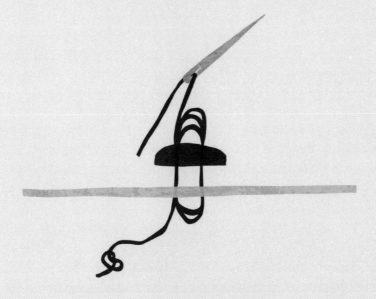

SEWING A BUTTON ONTO A LINED GARMENT

In jackets and coats that are lined, you don't really want to sew through all the layers of fabric and end up with an ugly knot on the inside of the garment. The solution is to tie a little knot on the thread and insert the needle about 1 cm (½ in.) away from the point where the button should sit.

YOU WILL NEED: *Needle. Thread to match the button.*

Bring the needle through to the point where the button should sit and then give a hard but firm little tug so that the knot on the thread disappears into the fabric. Then sew the button on, using stitches that pinch the garment's outer fabric but don't go all the way through to the lining. Keep the button about 1 cm (½ in.) away from the fabric as you sew. Wrap the thread around the shank and secure by sewing a couple of stitches through it, in the same way as when sewing a button onto an unlined garment.

If the fabric in the garment is thin or fragile, it can be a good idea to unpick the lining so that you can reach into the inside of the garment. Then you can sew on the button in the same way as for unlined garments, but using the stitches on the wrong side to secure a little button on the inside, meaning that you're sewing on two buttons at the same time! The little button on the inside doesn't need a shank and works as a weight distributor for the thread. In other words, it makes sure that the large button doesn't get torn off together with the thread and a piece of the garment's fabric.

GLUE RATHER THAN DOING NOTHING AT ALL

Textile glue might not be very highly regarded among mending purists, but it's actually incredibly effective when it comes to mending clothes. In the previous chapter I warned against using too much glue, but there are exceptions. A glued repair can never be completely removed – so if the garment is old and has a cultural or historic value, or if it feels wrong to ruin it for some other reason, you should perhaps not reach for the glue. But if it's working clothes we're talking about or some other everyday garment that isn't so precious – go for it! This method works for thicker fabrics such as jeans, jackets and thicker shirts.

YOU WILL NEED: *Textile glue. Fabric for a mending patch. Scissors.*

A textile that has been torn can never be repaired again using just textile glue; you need to support it with a patch as well. The patch can be placed on either the inside or the outside of the garment, but I recommend placing it on the inside because, when the glue eventually loses its strength and the patch becomes loose again, you can end up with visible stains from the glue.

Choose a fabric that is thinner than the one you are about to mend and cut out a patch about 1 cm (½ in.) bigger all around than the damaged area.

Brush glue thinly over the patch. If the patch will be visible through the hole, take care to avoid gluing the parts that will be seen. Stick the patch in place and wait a few minutes – and that's all there is to it!

REMOVING LINT BALLS WITH A RAZOR

It's not unusual for textiles to develop lint balls after a week or so of use. If the fabric is made of 100 per cent wool, be patient and wait a while; often the lint balls will wear off by themselves and won't return. Fabrics made from other materials, or wool mixed with something else (often acrylic, polyester or both) will develop lint balls that won't come off and then you'll have to resort to more drastic methods. You can remove lint balls from most textiles using a razor, as long as they're fairly firm. Loosely knitted jumpers and scarves are, unfortunately, beyond all salvation – unless you're happy to pick off the lint balls by hand.

YOU WILL NEED: *Manual razor.*

Stretch out the fabric by inserting your left hand into the garment. Use the palm of your hand as support and shave off the lint balls from the surface of the fabric, using light strokes as if you were buttering a slice of bread that you're holding in your hand. It's best to work in the direction of the fabric's fibre, if you can make it out.

SLIPSTITCHING A RIPPED SEAM

This is a good emergency mend for ripped seams – that is, when the thread that keeps a seam together has split. The mending is done from the outside of the garment, so it works particularly well for lined fabrics where, for example, you might not want to unpick the garment in order to reach the seam with a sewing machine.

YOU WILL NEED: *Thread. Needle.*

Start by tying a knot on one end of the thread and fasten it on the inside of the garment by inserting the needle through the hole that's created by the ripped seam. Bring the needle out approximately 1 cm (½ in.) away from where the seam has opened and right next to the seam, so that you pick up just a few threads from the fabric.

Sew the two pieces together using slipstitch, continuing for approximately 1 cm (½ in.) past the end of the hole to secure the thread of the ripped seam in place. Secure with two knots in the groove that appears around the seam, insert the needle and then bring it out again 2–3 cm (¾–1¼ in.) further away and pull tight, so that the knots are pulled through. Cut off the thread close to the fabric and the thread will disappear into the fabric.

THE PARACHUTE RANGERS' STITCH

My friend Johannes did his service for the Swedish Armed Forces with the Parachute Rangers and showed me this stitch, which was part of his training. It's a heavy-duty repair for situations where you need to solve the problem quickly! It's best suited for tears in materials such as tents, rucksacks, trousers, jackets or (why not?) parachutes.

When Johannes was taught this technique, all the soldiers were given a fabric patch with a tear in it, a needle and thread, and a picture with instructions for how to sew the repair. The officers then left the room, their parting words being that they would inspect the repairs the following morning. The inspection involved pulling the mend in order to judge whether it was properly executed and actually held together; those who failed simply had to repeat it until they passed the inspection.

YOU WILL NEED: *Thread, preferably a strong variety. Needle.*

Start by threading the needle and tying a knot at the end of the thread. Then bring the needle through from the wrong side of the fabric at the start of the tear, approximately 5 mm (¼ in.) away from the tear itself.

Start sewing by taking the needle through the tear and bringing it out through the fabric 5 mm (¼ in.) away from the other side of the tear. Pull the thread through and then do the exactly same thing but in the opposite direction, running the needle through the tear and out again 5 mm (¼ in.) away, just next to where you placed your first stitch. Continue sewing using the same technique. It's like sewing little figures of eight, where you always run the thread through the tear and up through the fabric on the opposite side.

Remember to never pull the thread tight, since the idea with this mend is to repair a material without pulling the fabric together or using a patch. The aim of this technique is to align the fabric's edges and stitch them together, not to make them overlap. The result is a strong mend that is quick to sew and suitable for emergencies!

MENDING
BY HAND

'Hand sewn' is a word that is used liberally today and can mean
many different things. For me it means sewing without a sewing
machine, using a needle and thread. Some might think that this
is a more primitive technique, but in fact a hand-sewn seam
can often be both stronger and neater than a seam sewn using a
sewing machine!

PATCH WITH FOLDED EDGES

When we tried this patching method for the first time, my partner Douglas exclaimed, 'It looks like a cartoon mend!'. The next day there was a customer in the shop who said the exact same thing, so now we call it 'the Donald Duck mend'.

YOU WILL NEED: *Scissors. Thick paper. Fabric for a mending patch. Needle. Thread. Iron. Pressing cloth. Pins (optional).*

Cut out a paper template the same shape you want the finished patch to be and 2 cm (¾ in.) larger all around than the hole or worn area. Place the paper template on the wrong side of the fabric you're using for the patch and tack (baste) it in place. Cut out a fabric patch, including a 1.5-cm (⅝-in.) seam allowance; in other words, the patch should be 1.5 cm (⅝ in.) larger all around than the paper template.

For a square patch, fold the seam allowance of the patch to the wrong side and press it flat.

For a round patch, gather the fabric by working long (5-mm/¼-in.) tacking stitches in the seam allowance and pulling the thread so that the edges of the patch close in over the paper template. Carefully press the edge to keep the rounded shape and continue all the way around the patch until the whole edge has been folded over to the wrong side.

Cut the thread that holds the paper template in place, take out the paper and press the front of the patch again. Tack or pin the patch in place on the garment and then sew the edges by hand or with a sewing machine.

SEWING ON ELBOW PATCHES

To patch the elbows of a knitted garment or jacket, you can use a felted wool fabric. There is a variety called 'broadcloth', which is so tightly felted that it won't fray. Cut out a piece to the required size and shape, tack it onto the garment and sew following the instructions above. You don't need to fold in the edges of the broadcloth; just sew on the patch using small, closely spaced stitches for a neat result.

PATCH WITH DOUBLE FOLDED EDGES

This is a mend that you will often find on older shirts. The advantage of this technique is that it looks just as good from both sides. It's important to keep to the grainline – that is, the direction of the threads in the fabric – for a neat end result.

YOU WILL NEED: *Iron. Pressing cloth. Scissors. Needle. Thread. Tacking thread. Tape measure. Fabric for a mending patch.*

Press the damaged area flat. Cut off all the damaged fabric so that you end up with a square or rectangular hole that follows the grain of the fabric. Make a 5-mm (¼-in.) long diagonal cut in each corner, fold the seam allowance over to the right side of the garment and tack (baste) down the edges (1). Press the edges flat. Measure how large the hole is now. Following the grain of the fabric, cut out a mending patch 1 cm (½ in.) larger all around than the hole. Fold, then tack the mending patch's edges to the wrong side by 5 mm (¼ in.). Press flat.

Now you should have a patch that exactly covers your rectangular hole. Place the patch over the hole on the right side of the garment, so that the tacked seam allowances cover each other, and tack in place (2).

Thread a needle and knot one end. Insert the needle in between the two tacked seam allowances and sew the patch to the garment using blind hem stitch (3). Turn the work over to the wrong side and sew the tacked edge around the hole to the back of the patch, again using blind hem stitch, so that both seam allowances cover each other. Remove the tacking threads and press.

1.   2.   3.

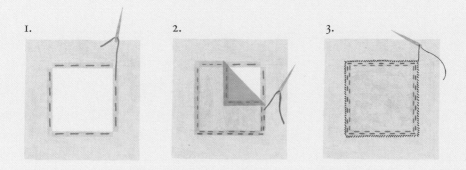

SEWING A BUTTONHOLE

A buttonhole is basically a hole in the fabric that has been hemmed with a row of stitches that reinforces the edges and stops them from fraying. These stitches can wear down if the buttonhole is exposed to a lot of strain. If you then continue to wear the garment, the fabric that was protected by the row of stitches will start to tear too and you will eventually end up with a frayed hole. Not much fun! This is how tailors sew a horizontal buttonhole, down to the smallest detail. You can choose yourself whether you want to follow the instructions to the letter or just pick out a few of the steps.

YOU WILL NEED: *Thread that is thicker than sewing thread, preferably silk buttonhole. Beeswax. Iron. Tracing paper or kitchen paper. Tailor's chalk. Sewing machine. Sewing machine thread. Sharp scissors with narrow tips. Hollow punch. Table knife. Needle.*

Measure out an arm's length of the thread that you are going to use for the buttonhole. Press the thread against the beeswax, running it back and forth a couple of times so that the whole thread comes in contact with the wax.

Set your iron to a warm (not hot) temperature. Place the thread between two pieces of tracing paper or kitchen paper and run your iron over the paper so that the wax melts into the thread.

Use tailor's chalk to mark the beginning and the end of the buttonhole. Using your sewing machine and a sewing machine thread that is as similar in colour to the fabric as possible, sew two parallel rows of stitches one on each side of the chalk marking.

Cut out the buttonhole in between the two rows of stitches, following the chalk marking. At the end of the buttonhole that is closest to the edge of the garment, punch out a round hole with your hollow punch.

Take out your table knife and hold the tip against the soleplate of the iron until it's really hot and then hold it against the beeswax so that it melts a little. Now you have to be quick and at the same time make sure you don't have too much wax on your knife, because before the wax sets you need to carefully insert the knife into the buttonhole to wax the edges. If you insert the knife from the back of the buttonhole, there's less chance that you will get wax stains on the front of the garment.

Once the buttonhole is waxed, it's time to start sewing. Thread the needle with a double length of the prepared waxed thread and knot the ends, then insert the needle into the fabric approximately 2 cm (¾ in.) away from the base of the buttonhole – that is, the edge furthest away from the garment's edge and the punched hole.Bring the needle through to the base of the buttonhole and sew with long stitches around the buttonhole, then bring the needle through to where you started and cut off one of the threads, leaving a 5-mm (¼-in.) tail. This thread is called the cord.

Sew buttonhole stitches (see page 44) in a row around the cord and the edge of the buttonhole. It's tempting to sew them so that they turn inwards towards the opening of the buttonhole – but don't do that! Aim the thread straight up when pulling the stitches so that they form a nice ridge all around the buttonhole. When you've come back around to the base of the buttonhole again, make two long stitches across the base and then two small stitches to secure them in place. Secure the thread on the reverse of the buttonhole by sewing a few small pick stitches next to the buttonhole stitches. You're done!

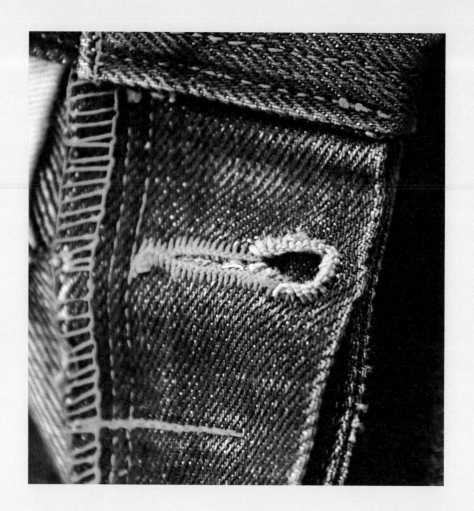

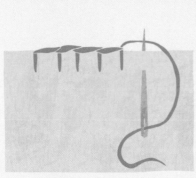

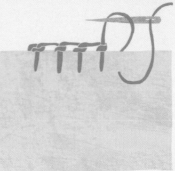

Blanket stitch.   *Buttonhole stitch.*

MENDING A BUTTONHOLE

If you've worn your jeans for a long time, you'll probably recognize this situation: eventually the button wears down the buttonhole and, if you're unlucky, the situation may quickly escalate and the whole waistband tear. This technique can be used for all sewn buttonholes, and it works just as well for jackets and coats as for jeans.

YOU WILL NEED: *Needle. Strong thread, preferably silk buttonhole. Beeswax. Iron. Tracing paper or kitchen paper.*

Start by removing all the old frayed buttonhole thread. If the fabric has frayed, too, you can reinforce it, as on page 47.

Then fill in with new cord by threading a needle with double waxed thread (as described in 'Sewing a buttonhole'), and inserting it so that it comes out through the old row of buttonhole stitches. Sew in the cord as if you were sewing a new buttonhole and insert the needle so that it slips in underneath the row of buttonhole stitches on the other side. Now bring the needle and thread through about 1–2 cm (½–¾ in.) away from the buttonhole and cut off so that you end up with a tail of thread about 2 cm (¾ in.) long that you leave hanging in case you need to tighten the thread.

Take a new waxed thread and secure with a few pick stitches on the reverse of the buttonhole. Bring the needle through to the row of buttonhole stitches so that you come out in between two knots, approximately 2–3 knots away from the place where the buttonhole stitches end, and then start sewing buttonhole stitches just as when you're sewing a completely new buttonhole. The first knots will then end up on top of the old ones, and it will then look like an unbroken chain.

Once you have worked your way to the other side of the buttonhole and want to merge with the old row of stitches, make a few buttonhole stitches over it and then insert the needle in between two knots. Secure on the reverse with a few pick stitches.

45

Reinforcing fabric

When you're thinking about patching something, the first thought that springs to mind is probably placing a patch on the outside of the garment. This type of patch is secured by sewing around the outside edges, and the patch itself creates a second layer of fabric on top of the damaged area. These type of repairs are good when the hole that needs fixing has appeared on a fabric that isn't fragile and worn (for example, if you got caught somewhere and the fabric got torn). However, if the fabric has worn thin or the garment has torn because the fabric has degraded, you can reinforce the area on the inside. This is also a good alternative if you prefer mends that are invisible, instead of patches that can be spotted a mile off.

In this technique, both the mending patch and the stitches are strengthening, and together they reinforce the damaged or worn fabric. The mending can be made more or less visible, depending on what thread and which stitches you use. The patch is placed on the inside of the fabric, so it will only be visible if the fabric has a hole in it.

PREPARATION

When choosing fabric for the mending patch, it's often a good idea to go for one that is thinner than the actual fabric of the garment – otherwise, the repair can end up like a hard cake when it's done.

Start by looking at the worn area of the garment: how big is it? You can assess how large the damaged area is by turning the garment inside out or holding it up to the light.

If possible, place the garment on top of an ironing board at this stage and press the worn area flat.

Then cut out a mending patch, making sure that it's slightly larger than the worn area; it's good to have a margin of 1–2 cm (½–¾ in.). Also make sure that the grainline of the patch corresponds to the grainline of the fabric, otherwise there's a chance that the mending patch will pucker after washing.

Now it's time to secure the patch in place on the wrong side of the garment. I tend to go for textile glue here. Dab a little bit of glue along the edge of the worn area and place the patch on top; it will fix in a few seconds. If you use too much glue, it will go through the fabric and create stains on the right side of the garment, so take it easy!

If the fabric is thin (as on a shirt, for example), it's almost impossible to avoid glue stains. In this case, I recommend tacking (basting) instead; it's a bit more fiddly but will look better.

Once the patch is in place, it's time to sew!

HAND-SEWN REINFORCEMENT

A hand-sewn reinforcement can be varied more in its appearance than a machine-sewn one, since you have more choice of thread when sewing by hand than you do when sewing by machine. Another bonus is that hand-sewn reinforcements are often more flexible than those sewn on a machine, probably because the stitches don't end up as tight.

When sewing by hand you have the opportunity to vary your stitches to infinity, and there is an enormous world of embroidery techniques to take inspiration from. I have opted for the simplest stitch of them all – running stitch. The stitches on their own aren't that special; the challenge lies instead in placing them in relation to each other to create different patterns and textures.

I think that the stitches should be fairly evenly spaced over the surface of the fabric, so that they reinforce the whole area that is to be mended. It's important to use thread that's a little bit thicker than standard sewing thread, so that it fills out the stitches nicely. I prefer to sew with a thick, soft weaving yarn made from cotton that I bought at a flea market, which makes both soft and comfortable repairs and fills out the stitches.

REINFORCING WITH RUNNING STITCH

Secure the thread by reverse stitching and bring the needle through to the right side of the fabric. Now cover the whole surface with tiny, tiny running stitches. Ideally, they shouldn't be longer than 2–3 mm (⅛ in. or less) and they should sit very close together to create that crowded feeling. Here are some tips to help you make the end result as good as possible.

Don't pull the stitches too tight! It's easy to believe that it's important to pull the stitches tight to make the mending strong. But the result will actually be better if each stitch is allowed to sit over the fabric like a thick little grain of rice. It will become strong anyway.

Only make one stitch at a time – that is, insert the needle through the fabric, pull it out on the reverse and then run it through the fabric from the reverse side again. In the interests of efficiency, you might be tempted to sew several running stitches in one go by inserting the needle into the fabric and then up again a bit further away before pulling it all the way through, but in my experience this results in little stitches that are pulled too tight; this will eventually pucker the whole fabric and it can become difficult to work through all the layers.

When the thread is coming to an end, reverse stitch to secure the old thread and to start the new one. It's not comfortable to have lumpy knots in the inside of a garment!

The reinforcement shown opposite is sewn in straight lines, but you can just as well start in the middle of the patch and work your way out in a spiral. If you do, it's extra important not to pull the stitches too tight, because the mending will pull the fabric together to create a little cone with the middle of your spiral on the top.

INVISIBLE REINFORCEMENT SEWN BY HAND

If you don't want the reinforcement to be seen, you can use a thin sewing thread and sew with small stitches that are almost invisible from the outside of the garment. This kind of reinforcement isn't as durable in the long run, but it does the job for torn garments that you are not ready to let go of just yet.

This reinforcement is basically sewn in the same way as a visible hand-sewn reinforcement, but with a few differences:

– Choose a thin thread instead of a thick one.

– Use a patch that is as thin and supple as possible. Thin silk is good, or a cotton fabric that is so thin that you can see through it.

– Sew using small pick stitches that are placed approximately 8–10 mm (⅜–½ in.) apart. Secure with little knots instead of reverse stitching, otherwise thin sewing threads can easily become undone.

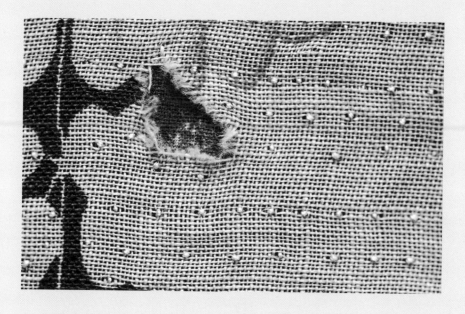

My favourite dressing gown got ripped over the shoulders, and was given support in the form of a blue patterned cotton fabric. Now it will last for a while longer!

PATCHING A BACK POCKET FROM THE INSIDE

If you have a hole on the back pocket of your jeans, there are a few different ways to tackle the problem, and the hand-sewn technique is actually quicker than the sewing-machine technique!

The easiest way is to cut out a patch approximately 2 cm (¾ in.) larger than the hole, which you fix in place on the inside of the pocket using textile glue. Sew the hole's edges in place with blind hem stitch and then sew two rows of closely spaced running stitches around the edges of the hole to secure the patch.

If you don't want to sew by hand, you will have to unpick the pocket until you can reach in and reinforce the hole using your sewing machine (see page 80) and then sew the pocket back in place again. You will probably not have to remove the whole pocket, but to be able to fit it onto the machine relatively easily, you usually need to unpick a substantial part of the seam.

Once the reinforcement is done and you need to sew the pocket back on again, you can usually see on the jeans exactly where the pocket used to sit, so it's easy to pin it in place and sew it on again. It's best to use a slightly thicker top thread for your sewing machine (see page 82) when sewing on the pocket to make the seam look as similar to the original one as possible.

53

Sashiko

Sashiko is a Japanese sewing technique that was traditionally used to reinforce, mend or sew together one or several layers of fabric. The technique is built up of rows of running stitch that form different patterns. There are many different branches within sashiko. What they have in common is that they are very rarely figurative, but instead are built up over large areas of geometric shapes.

Sashiko is often sewn with white cotton thread on indigo-dyed cotton or hemp, but there are colour variations both on new objects and on old examples that can be found in museums all over the world.

I take a lot of inspiration from this tradition, which is circumscribed by a lot of rules, despite it looking very simple at first sight. Therefore I have chosen to interpret sashiko in my own way, instead of strictly keeping to the traditional styles.

It can be difficult to get a nice and relaxed look when working only with running stitch, and the trick is to not rush! Long, sprawled stitches reveal that the person who made them worked too quickly, focusing on finishing off the work rather than making it as good as possible, and this is not an attitude that goes very well with sashiko.

SHIRT ARM WITH GRID

Behind the fragile fabric on the shirt's elbow, I tacked (basted) down a patch made from thin cotton fabric, and then sewed rows of running stitch to secure the patch in place. The thread itself contributes as much to the reinforcement as the actual patch.

YOU WILL NEED: *Thread that is thicker than sewing thread. Needle with a large eye.*

Secure the thread by reverse stitching in one of the corners of the area that you want to reinforce, and then cover the area with horizontal rows of running stitch. After this you can sew more rows of stitches placed at an angle to the first ones, until you're happy with the result. For the shirt shown opposite, I worked three layers of stitches in total.

FISHBONE PATTERN

I thought for a long time how to make this mend work. On my initial test patch, I soon lost the momentum: the stitches became uneven and the rows became too sparse at first and then too narrow. I ditched the idea and started on another sashiko variety instead – but when the first layer of stitches was complete, I realized that it was the perfect base onto which to sew a fishbone pattern.

The mending in the photo opposite was done over a tear on a trouser knee and I did some reinforcing work before starting with the visible stitches.

The damaged area was pressed flat and the edges of the tear were placed against each other. A thin piece of linen fabric was tacked (basted) in place behind the tear and then I sewed down the tear's edges, using a linen thread that was so similar to the trouser fabric that it became almost invisible. I used the Parachute Rangers' stitch (see page 34), but I also let the needle run through the linen fabric behind the tear, which prevented it from opening up during the course of the stitching.

YOU WILL NEED: *Thread that is thicker than sewing thread. Needle with a large eye. Tailor's chalk or pencil (optional).*

The stitches in this pattern are, as mentioned, sewn in two stages: first you sew half of the stitches and then you sew the rest of the stitches in between the first.

Secure the thread by reverse stitching in the lower left corner of the area that you want to reinforce. Then sew a row of stitches that are about the same distance apart as the stitches are long. When it's time to sew the next row, place it about one stitch's length away from the first row. The stitches in the second row should be offset in relation to the stitches in the first row (1).

Cover the whole area with this type of stitch rows. It can be a bit tricky to keep the distance in between the rows even, and a tip is to carefully mark lines with chalk or pencil to use as a guide. When the thread is almost used up, reverse stitch to secure the old thread and to start the new one.

When it's time to fill in with the second layer of stitches (2), it can be a bit tricky to put the stitches in the right place at first – but have a think about how it's all going to come together and you'll soon be able to get going!

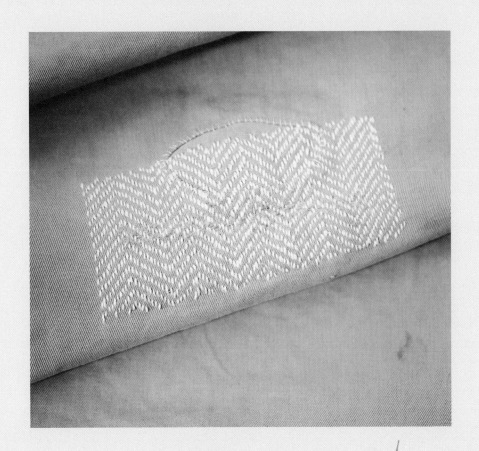

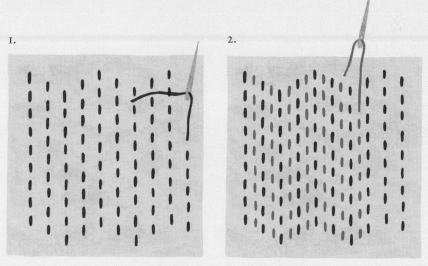

1.

2.

PATCHED KNEE WITH SASHIKO STITCHING AND INDIGO-DYED FABRIC

These old jeans were worn thin over the knee and it felt like the perfect opportunity to make a truly striking mend! The pattern is sewn with cotton weaving yarn over a piece of indigo-dyed cotton fabric.

YOU WILL NEED: *Scissors. Tailor's chalk. Ruler. Thread that is thicker than sewing thread. Needle with a large eye.*

Start by cutting out a piece of fabric 1 cm (½ in.) larger all around than the area that you want to mend. It's a good idea to mark up the seam allowance with tailor's chalk, so that you know which area to fit the pattern onto.

Using your tailor's chalk and a ruler, mark up the pattern you want to sew. When the pattern is detailed, like this one, it's best to mark up and sew the basic structure first, and then mark up and sew the rest. If you mark everything in one go, the lines can get blurred when you start sewing.

For this pattern, it's easiest to mark up the diagonal lines first so that you get a diamond pattern. Once you have covered these lines with stitches, you can mark up the pattern that is going to fill the diamonds.

Before you start filling in the pattern with stitches, however, you will need to secure the patch in place on the fabric that it is to reinforce. Fold under the edges of the patch and tack (baste) in place, following the instructions for 'Patch with folded edges' (see page 38).

Then you can start sewing. Use running stitch and reverse stitch to secure the thread. Start by sewing down the edges of the patch, and then remove the tacking thread. Once you have sewn down the edges, continue with the diagonal lines, and when the whole patch is covered with diamonds, mark up new lines to fill in the pattern inside the diamonds. Remember not to make your stitches too long. It also looks best if you don't let the stitches cross over each other. The stitches at the corners of the patch will look good if you insert the needle in the middle of the corner and let the next stitch come out a stitch length away on the next row.

LITTLE LEAVES

I saw this pattern on an old Japanese fabric and I think it's beautiful in its simplicity. It's built up from two layers: first you make a grid, then you fill the squares of the grid with leaf shapes. I tend to want to make everything as little as possible, but if you sew the grid too small it will be difficult to fit the leaves inside, so I sketched out the pattern on a piece of paper first to make sure that everything would fit. The jacket arm was ripped across the elbow, so I tacked (basted) a piece of a worn-out shirt on the inside of the damaged and fragile fabric to reinforce it. I secured the frayed edges of the hole with blind hem stitch before I started sewing the actual pattern.

YOU WILL NEED: *Tailor's chalk. Ruler. Needle. Thread.*

If you want, you can work out how large the squares in the grid should be, mark them up with tailor's chalk and a ruler and then fill them in. I estimated the size and started by marking up the vertical lines. I filled them in with stitches and then marked up and sewed the horizontal lines. The main thing is that you make a grid with squares over the area that you want to reinforce! Use running stitch and reverse stitch to secure the thread for a neat result.

Once your grid is complete, you can mark up diagonal lines through the squares that you then fill with leaf shapes. Perfectionists can mark up the exact rounding of the leaves, but you will get a nice result if you sew them freehand, too!

DARNING

Few things are as satisfying as sewing new threads into a fabric and seeing a hole slowly disappear. I think it's most fun to darn with a coarse thread that is very visible.

CLASSIC DARNING

This technique is usually associated with mending knitted socks, but it can also be used for woven fabrics. Traditionally, darning is built up by sewing threads vertically over the whole area that is to be mended (of course, you could start by sewing horizontally – but for the sake of making the instructions simpler, I suggest vertical stitches), and then filling in with horizontal stitches. The horizontal stitches will alternate between going over and under the vertical threads and this way the result will appear woven.

Start by choosing your thread. Remember that it will be very visible, so either pick a thread that you think is nice and that you want to stand out or one that is as close to the colour of the fabric as possible if you don't want it to be as noticeable. Choose a thread that is slightly thicker than your gut feeling tells you to use; it will usually pay off later.

To prevent the darning puckering around the surrounding fabric, it's good to stretch out the fabric around the hole with something. If the garment is large enough to stretch out in an embroidery hoop, that will work well – but if the garment is a small item like a sock, for example, you could use a darning mushroom instead. (A darning mushroom looks like a mushroom made out of wood. Over the mushroom's cap you stretch out the part of the fabric that you are about to mend by inserting the mushroom into the garment, centre the hole and then grip around the mushroom's stalk and the surrounding fabric.)

If the hole is smaller than about 1 cm (½ in.), I usually don't bother stretching it; you can choose yourself how meticulous you want to be.

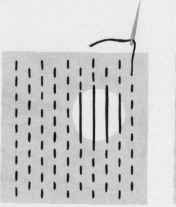 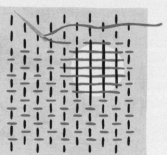

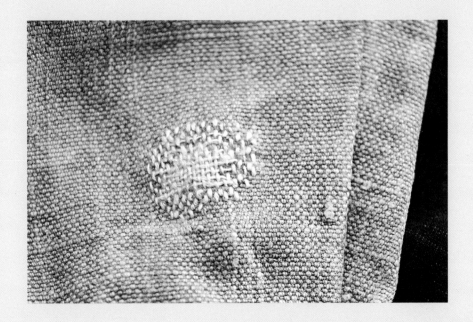

YOU WILL NEED: *Thread or yarn, depending on the fabric that you are mending. Needle. Darning mushroom or embroidery hoop (if necessary).*

Decide the size of the area you want to darn. Secure the thread by reverse stitching, and then cover the surface with vertical stitches that are as long as the spaces in between them. The trick is to offset the rows instead of aligning them, so that the stitches form a pattern like rows of bricks (see opposite). When you come to the damaged area, take the needle over the hole to the other side, where you continue to sew. Work your way across the whole surface that you want to darn, so that it's covered with parallel stitches. Be careful not to pull the thread too tight; instead, let it sit softly over the surface of the fabric.

When you have made rows of stitches all over the area, start filling in with the horizontal rows. Place a stitch in each gap that has appeared between the vertical threads; when you come to the long threads that run across the hole, take the thread under the first thread and over the next, and so on until you reach the other side. When you're done, reverse stitch to secure the thread.

BLANKET STITCH DARNING

This darning is suitable for most materials, and I have used it for both woven fabrics and knitted sock heels. It won't become elastic, but it doesn't matter so much since the rest of the sock usually compensates a little if necessary.

    Blanket stitch darning is built up from stitches that are sewn into each other to create a net-like structure. I use it primarily for filling in holes on textiles and regard it as a more decorative alternative to a traditional darn. You will get the best result if you sew it with a relatively thin thread, but it can take an awful amount of time to fill in a large hole. My solution to the problem is to let an extra thread run in between the stitches as a filler. However, if you want the mending to be as thin and flexible as possible, you can skip the filler thread completely and build up the mending from just blanket stitches.

YOU WILL NEED: *Scissors. Needle. Thread (fairly thin, but thicker than sewing thread). Filler thread (optional). Darning mushroom or embroidery hoop (if necessary). Iron. Pressing cloth.*

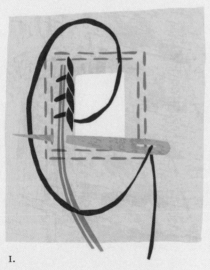 

I.   2.

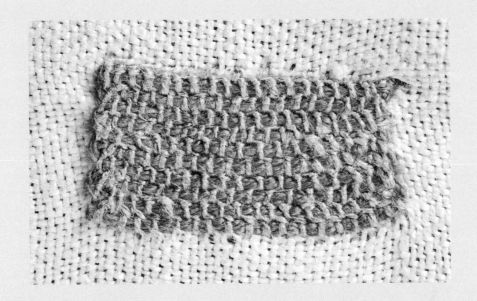

Start by cutting off all the damaged material around the hole and cut it out to make it rectangular. Sew two rows of running stitch around the edges of the hole. These will act as a reinforcement and prevent the edges from fraying during the next step. These threads don't need securing.

Secure the filler thread, if using, by reverse stitching just inside the top left corner of the edge reinforcement. Secure the thread that you are sewing with by means of a small knot on the inside of the garment and bring the needle back up right next to the filler thread. Sew blanket stitches around both the running-stitch edge reinforcement and the filler thread (1). Work your way down to the bottom left corner of the hole. When you have sewn over the edge reinforcement's bottom left corner, insert the needle right next to your last blanket stitch. This marks the end of the first row.

Bring the needle back up through your last blanket stitch and start working your way back up to the top left of the hole. Every stitch you just made will leave a small hoop that you can pick up and attach the next row of stitches to, and you will get a neat result if you are careful to pick up all the hoops (2).

When you have covered all of the hole with stitches, check to see if the last row of blanket stitches has formed a small, hard strip at the upper edge of the darning. If it has, sew it down in place against the fabric using blind hem stitch. For best results, press the finished mend.

SCOTCH DARNING

I fell for this mending technique straight away when I saw it on the Internet a few years ago. It's best suited to small holes that have appeared on fabrics – for example, if vermin have helped themselves to a bite from a table cloth. Textiles that are worn thin around the hole will give too little support for this darning.

YOU WILL NEED: *Scissors. Needle. Thread (fairly thin, but thicker than sewing thread). Darning mushroom or embroidery hoop (if necessary). Iron. Pressing cloth.*

Start by cutting off the damaged edges around the hole and shape the hole to make it round. Sew two rows of running stitch around the edges of the hole. These will add strength and prevent the edges from fraying during the next step.

Stretch the fabric over an embroidery hoop or a darning mushroom if you think it's necessary. Sew a close round of blanket stitches around the edge of the hole (1). When the circle is complete, start working buttonhole stitches into the previous round of blanket stitches (2). Each stitch will leave a small loop at the edge that you can pick up and attach the next row's stitches to. Skip every third or fourth loop, or you will end up with a dome shape! When you get to the middle, push the needle through to the wrong side and secure the thread. Press the finished mend to make it nice and flat.

I.

2.

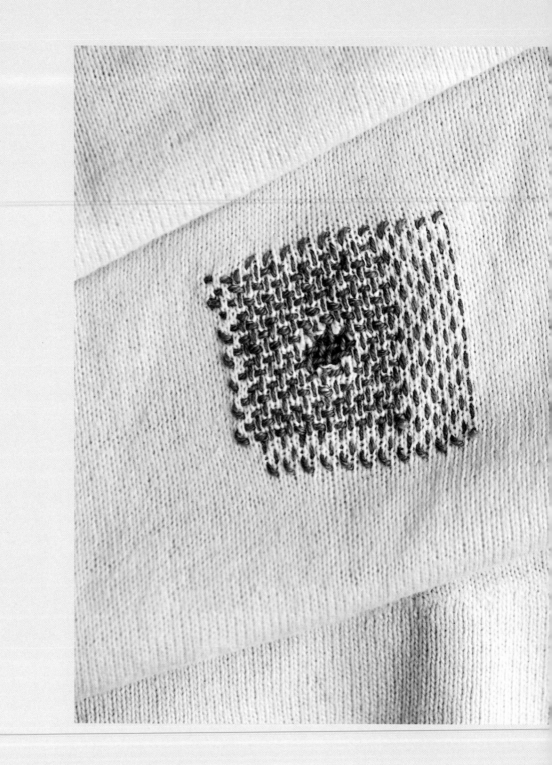

MENDING KNIT FABRICS

It's generally quite difficult to make durable repairs on garments made from knit fabrics, especially newly produced garments where the stitches are so ridiculously tiny that you can barely see them. But there might be occasions where you've used your coolest T-shirt until it has ripped and you simply can't bear to part with it. This is my method if you want to give a knit fabric a second chance.

The most important thing to keep in mind when mending knit materials is that the fabric you are mending will stretch – so the mending patch and the seams need to be able to stretch as well. Find a fabric that is as similar as possible to the one you want to mend in terms of both stretchiness and thickness, and then decide whether you want to place the patch on the outside or the inside of the garment. I recommend sewing the patch on by hand, but I've also noted down what I know about mending knit fabrics using the sewing machine.

SEWING ON A MACHINE

Set the sewing machine to zigzag stitch. Pin or tack (baste) the patch in place and then sew along the edges of the patch. It's important not to pull the fabric and it's good to use a special ballpoint needle if the fabric is thin. (A ballpoint needle has a rounded tip that is designed to slip in between the stitches of the fabric instead of tearing them apart, and can be found in haberdasheries.)

SEWING BY HAND

Pin or tack the patch in place. Select a thread that is thicker than standard sewing thread; cotton embroidery thread is good. Sew the patch in place using narrowly spaced catch stitch, which will become stretchy, since the thread is run diagonally over the edge of the patch. Don't pull your catch stitches too tight or the mend will pucker; the stitches shouldn't be too loose, either. If you can't be bothered to go out and buy embroidery thread and want to use whatever sewing thread you have at home – don't! If this kind of seam is sewn with a thin polyester thread, it will easily tear when the garment is used. Polyester thread is easy to sew with, but in this context it's not a good choice.

DARNING KNIT FABRICS

Sometimes people come into our store with clothes they wonder if we can sell. When the '50s T-shirt (see pages 66–67) came in, we didn't notice it had been mended, but just as we were about to hang it out in the shop we paused. The T-shirt ended up in our own collection instead, because on closer inspection we noticed it had been carefully reinforced at the neck with a darning in soft, white cotton yarn. And here I was thinking that you couldn't darn knit fabrics! Apparently it can be done very well. The darning itself isn't very stretchy, but it doesn't matter so much since the surrounding fabric still can move and stretch a little extra and therefore compensate for the stiff darning.

YOU WILL NEED: *Darning needle. Yarn for darning.*

This is similar to a classic darning, apart from it being sewn over counted threads. If you look really carefully, you will see that knit fabrics are made out of stitches – and you can count these if you want your own stitches to be the exact same size! In the example below, I have sewn over two and under two stitches.

Secure your darning yarn by reverse stitching, and then sew all the vertical stitches, leaving an empty row of stitches in between each row.

Then sew all the horizontal stitches, being careful to take the thread over and under alternate stitches when you come to the place where there's a hole in the fabric. For a neat finish, secure the end of an old thread or the start of a new thread by reverse stitching.

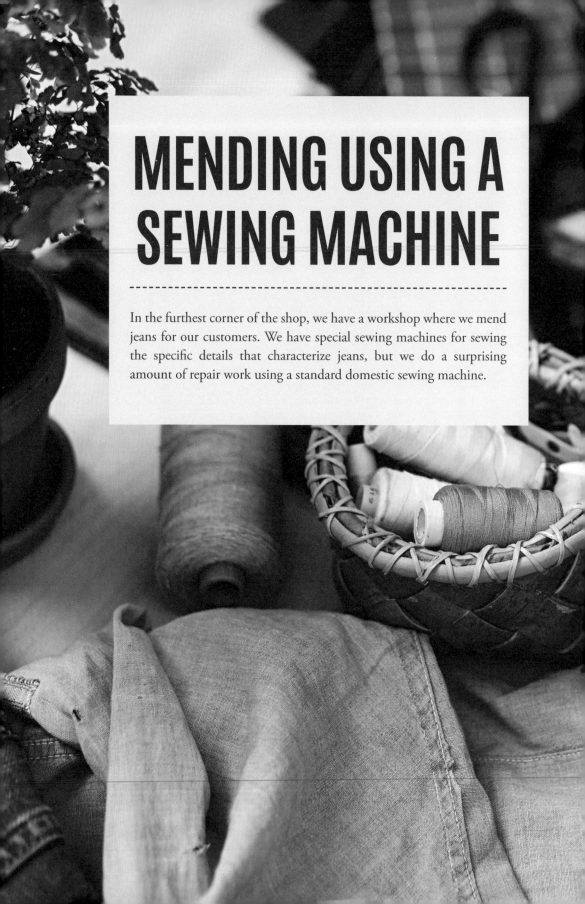

MENDING USING A SEWING MACHINE

In the furthest corner of the shop, we have a workshop where we mend jeans for our customers. We have special sewing machines for sewing the specific details that characterize jeans, but we do a surprising amount of repair work using a standard domestic sewing machine.

REINFORCING USING A SEWING MACHINE

Many people will recognize the problem of jeans that get worn at the crotch and on the knees, and for that type of wear I recommend this technique. This is the repair that I use the most, and our favourite technique when it comes to mending jeans. It's quick, durable and can be made almost invisible.

YOU WILL NEED: *Mending patch. Sewing machine. Sewing machine thread.*

A hole at the crotch of a pair of trousers can easily be reached using a sewing machine, but if you are mending a hole on an arm or a knee start by checking to see if there are any seams in the vicinity that you can unpick to make it easier to coax the work onto the machine. It can feel drastic to open up the garment, but it will usually save you a lot of time in the long run. Of course, it is possible to thread a trouser leg onto the sewing machine to reach the knee – but I've learned the hard way that it often leads to the surrounding fabric getting sewn down by mistake, and the time that you then have to spend unpicking could be used for something more fun!

Start by placing a patch behind the damaged area (see page 46). Now decide what direction you want the stitches to run. I usually follow the weave in the direction of the warp threads (1 – the blue threads in a jeans fabric), but there are different schools of thought. Many people choose instead to sew the stitches in the direction of the diagonal rib that appears in twill woven fabrics (2). Test both to decide which option you prefer.

Now you can start sewing. Here I have placed narrowly spaced rows of stitches next to each other, following the warp of the fabric. Start sewing outside of the top left edge of the mending patch and then work using long, narrow stitches by sewing straight ahead and then, on the next row, reversing over the area that you want to reinforce. Make sure that the area that you cover with stitches is slightly larger than the mending patch that sits on the inside, so that the stitches hold the edges of the patch in place. Finish off by securing the thread, cut off all the loose threads and sew the garment back together again, if you had to unpick a seam.

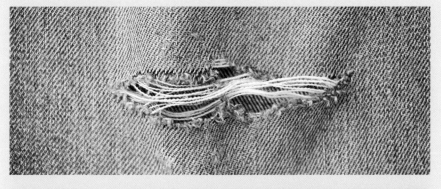

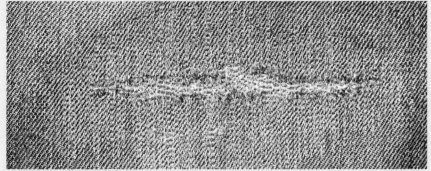

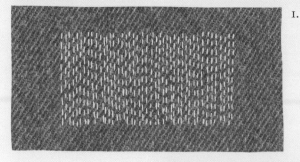

1.

2.

REINFORCING USING THICK THREAD

There are occasions where you will want to swap the sewing machine thread for a slightly thicker thread when mending on a sewing machine. Perhaps you want the mending to be more visible or the fabric is woven from thick threads, meaning that a coarser thread will be suitable.

If you've tried to thread a domestic sewing machine with extra-thick thread, you've probably experienced the thread getting stuck in the machine and forming knots. If not – congratulations! Ignore the following advice. For everyone else, my tip is to use the thicker thread just for the top thread. Wind the bobbin with standard sewing machine thread in the same colour (or similar) as the thick thread. Take care when sewing, and you will see (and hear!) if the sewing machine accepts the arrangement. To make the stitches extra neat, you might need to tighten the bobbin thread a little to compensate for the thickness of the top thread.

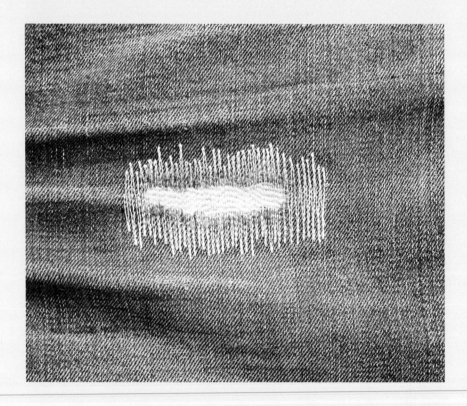

MENDING HOLES ON ROLLED-UP JEANS

If you prefer to wear your jeans with the legs rolled up, you'll notice that the fabric tends to get worn at the fold after a while. When I mend this kind of hole, I don't place a patch on the inside of the trousers, since this is what becomes visible when the leg is rolled up. Instead, I place the patch on the outside of the trousers. A thin jeans fabric is the best option for mending, but a cotton fabric in a similar colour to the right side of the trousers will work, too. To avoid this type of hole, roll down and clean the fold from time to time. Usually these holes are caused from grit and little stones that end up in the fold, which will wear down the fibres over time.

YOU WILL NEED: *Iron. Scissors. Fabric for a patch. Textile glue. Sewing machine. Sewing machine thread.*

Start by unrolling the fold and then iron out the crease so that the trousers are as flat as possible. Arrange the fabric surrounding the hole so that it looks like it's in the same position as it was before the hole appeared. Then cut out a piece of fabric that is slightly larger than the hole, place it in position with the right side facing up and glue in place with a little bit of textile glue.

Thread the sewing machine with a top thread that matches the blue colour of the right side of the jeans and a bobbin thread that matches the colour of the wrong side of the jeans. Usually I go for a grey thread here, since a white thread will appear too white and a blue thread won't blend in at all.

Sew the patch in place from the right side with narrowly spaced rows of straight stitch, as described in 'Reinforcing using a sewing machine' (see page 80). Make sure that the rows of stitches extend beyond the mending patch. While you're at it, take the opportunity to check if the fabric is worn in any other places around the fold line; often holes develop in several places at once. If the fabric is just worn but not ripped, you don't need to add a mending patch; a few extra stitches for reinforcement will do the job.

1.

2.

MENDING POCKETS

As you probably already know, pockets are usually made from a thinner fabric to the rest of the garment. When it comes to jeans it was fairly common during the nineteenth century to make the pockets in the same fabric as the actual trousers. These heavy-duty pockets were more durable than today's thinner pockets, although thick pockets make the trousers more uncomfortable – so with time, durability has been pushed aside in favour of comfort.

It's common for the pocket to give up sooner than the rest of the trousers, and it can be frustrating to put your keys in your pocket just to feel them pass through a hole and slide down your leg. But there are simple tricks to quickly and efficiently mend pockets.

YOU WILL NEED: *Sewing machine. Sewing machine thread. Scissors. Textile glue (if necessary). Fabric for a patch (if necessary).*

If there is a hole in the bottom edge of the pocket, the easiest way to mend it is just to trim it off. Sew a seam straight across the pocket above the hole and then cut off the bottom, ripped part of the pocket. Neaten the raw edge with a zigzag seam, and the fabric won't fray.

Sometimes the pocket will rip at the top edge, just where you insert your hands. If the hole isn't too big, you can glue the pocket's fabric against the inside of the trouser fabric and then sew it in place with straight stitch using a sewing machine, similar to reinforcing using a sewing machine (see page 80). It can be tricky to reach through the pocket opening, but with a bit of willpower it's possible. Work from the outside of the trousers and sew across the whole area that needs to be secured in place.

If the lower part of the pocket is worn thin and has several holes, it may be time to replace part of it. Cut off the damaged part of the pocket in a straight line just above the damaged area and then unpick 2 cm (¾ in.) or so of the pocket's side seam (1). Take out the fabric you are using for mending and use the cut-off piece as a template to cut out the piece that is going to be your new pocket. Remember to add a seam allowance!

Sew the patch in place along the bottom edges of the old pocket. It also looks good – and is more durable – if you zigzag the two pieces of fabric together and topstitch the edge (2).

To finish off, sew the new pocket's bottom edge with straight stitch and zigzag the raw edges of the old and new pocket pieces together. If you want to make it extra fancy, turn the pocket inside out to sew it together. When you then turn it right side out again, the seam allowance will end up inside the pocket, and to prevent it from fraying or wearing down from sharp keys, you can sew a seam along the edge of the pocket. This means that the seam allowance is enclosed and protected. This is how I made the pocket pictured below (3).

If the pockets are so damaged that none of the above mending techniques will be enough, the whole pocket might need replacing. This requires advanced sewing skills, and sometimes certain specialist tools, so in this case I recommend taking it to a tailor to get it fixed. It might cost you a bit, but it can be cheaper than buying a completely new garment.

3.

MENDING KNITS

When I was a child, the soft presents were the least appealing ones under the Christmas tree, but now, 20 years later, the last pair of knitted socks from grandma takes the place of honour in the wardrobe. Nothing lasts forever, not even grandma's socks, but with knitted repairs you can make them last for a good long time.

The distinguishing feature of a knitted material is that it is built up of threads that run across in loops, called 'stitches', that hook into each other, as opposed to woven fabrics where the threads overlap each other without forming loops. This means that knitted materials are more stretchy than woven materials, but it also means that they can unravel in a completely different way to a woven fabric. If a thread has split, the loops will start to unravel in all directions possible! Luckily there are a range of tricks for fishing them up again, and it's actually possible to make an almost invisible mend on knitted garments if you can get hold of a thread similar to the one the fabric is made from.

Most of the mending techniques in this book can be used also for knitted garments if it's not important whether the mending is stretchy or not, but if you think it matters, there are some special repairs for knits on the following pages.

SWISS DARNING

The area of a knitted garment that is exposed to the most amount of wear will sooner or later become worn down, but if you're lucky enough to discover it before a hole has developed you can actually reinforce the garment by sewing new yarn into the stitches of the worn areas. Try to always use yarn that is slightly thinner than the one the garment is made from, otherwise the mending will get thick and heavy.

YOU WILL NEED: *Darning needle. Yarn. Iron. Pressing cloth.*

The mending is sewn in horizontal rows, and in this case I have worked from left to right. Secure the yarn by going through the back of the first three stitches that you are filling in, and then start working over the stitches of the original garment (see page 95). When you reach the end of the row and no longer want to continue further to the right, push the needle though to the inside of the garment and bring it back through to the start of the new row, at the left-hand side of the work. If you skip more than four stitches on your way back, you will get a long thread that can easily get caught later when you are wearing the garment. To avoid the problem, slip the thread through a thread on the inside of the garment on your way back to the left-hand side.

Before you start a new left-hand row, it's a good idea to pull the work sideways a little bit, so that the yarn is fully stretched out.

You can, of course, sew from left to right and then back again from right to left, and your work will get less thick. But I think the yarn tends to twist when doing it this way, so I prefer to sew from left to right. Do test out both ways!

When it's time to secure your work, just sew the end of the yarn into the work with a few stitches on the inside; you don't need to make any knots.

The most important thing to keep in mind when sewing Swiss darning is to not pull too tight, but not make it too loose either. The stitches should sit as a soft arm around the shoulders of the stitches of the original garment. When the mending is completed, you can press it with a damp pressing cloth and it will sink in nicely into the surrounding fabric.

PATTERNED SWISS DARNING

This is the slightly more show-off version of a Swiss darning mend. Patterned Swiss darning can be used to mend a patterned garment or to make a patterned mend on a plain garment. It can look very striking! The technique is executed in the same way as normal Swiss darning, but with more colours of yarn. For this cardigan I worked the orange stitches first and then filled up with white. Finally, I sewed in the yellow stitches.

Swiss darning is particularly suitable for making invisible mendings. If you choose a yarn in the same colour as the garment, the mending can be made almost invisible, – but if you choose yarn in a contrasting colour, it will become a bit more visible. You can also use Swiss darning for sewing purely decorative patterns on a knitted garment – for example, if you want a jumper with a special text on.

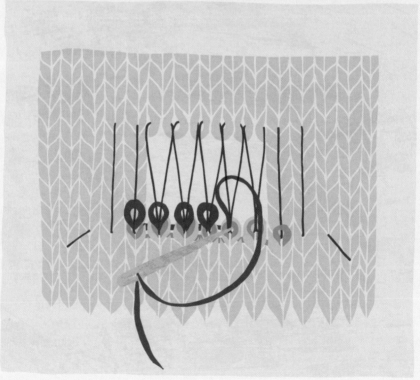

SWISS DARNING WITH SUPPORT THREADS

If you want to mend a hole on a knitted garment you can weave support threads over the hole and sew Swiss darning stitches over them. It's pretty tricky to get the right tension and it might be best to sew the rows from left to right instead of working back and forth. Test it out over a small hole before tackling a large one.

YOU WILL NEED: *Scissors. Embroidery hoop or hard card. Support thread – for example, sewing thread in a contrasting colour that's easy to see. Needle. Button. Darning needle. Yarn, slightly thinner than the yarn of the original garment. Iron. Pressing cloth.*

Start by cutting the hole clean of loosely hanging yarn threads. Then fix the area that you are mending by stretching it out – for example, in an embroidery hoop or by tacking (basting) it onto hard card. Thread your support thread onto the needle and tie a little button to one end. Secure by inserting the needle a few centimetres (½ in. or so) away from the area that you are working and bring it through right in the middle of the last whole row of stitches before the hole starts. The button will work like a knot, so that the end of the support thread doesn't slide through the knitted material. Now start sewing in the support threads, as in the illustration. Try to keep the tension even over the whole area. Pull the thread fairly tight, but not so tight that the hole is pulled together.

When the support threads are in place, it's time to start the actual mending. Thread a darning needle with the yarn you're using for the Swiss darning. Start by making a few stitches outside the bottom left corner of the hole and sew Swiss darning stitches, following the instructions on page 93, until you reach the hole itself. Now it can feel as if you're standing on the edge of an abyss – but keep a cool head and think about how the Swiss darning stitches are sewn and it will be okay! When you've started sewing stitches around the support threads, remember not to pull them too tight and that if you catch a little bit of the yarn of the previous stitch it will be easier to get to grips with it all. When the whole hole and a few rows of stitches outside of it are covered, secure the thread by running it through a few threads at the back of the work and cut it off. Then you can pick out the support threads and press flat.

PICKING UP UNRAVELLED STITCHES

Knit fabrics are built up of yarn that runs in horizontal lines and forms stitches that are vertically linked to each other. If a yarn thread in a knitted material splits, the stitches can start to unravel vertically – a real classic when it comes to tights, where you get a little hole that results in the stitches above and below unravelling at incredible speed. It might be a bit too complex to mend tights using this method, but a jumper where one or a couple of stitches have unravelled can easily be saved.

YOU WILL NEED: *Crochet hook.*

Start by looking at the point where the ladder ends; this is where you will find the last row of unravelled stitches. To understand how they hook into each other, grip the fabric on either side of the unravelled stitch and pull the fabric gently. When you do this, the stitch will unravel further and you get a chance to study how it's all joined together. It can feel a little scary, but it's nothing to worry about!

Thereafter you can insert the crochet hook into the stitch that is next in line to unravel. Hook into the horizontal thread right above it, pull it through the loop of the stitch and voila: you have a new loop to hook the next horizontal thread into. Work your way to where the damage occurred; there you can secure the final stitch. Use a few Swiss darning stitches (see page 95) or a piece of yarn that runs through the stitch and secure on the inside of the fabric.

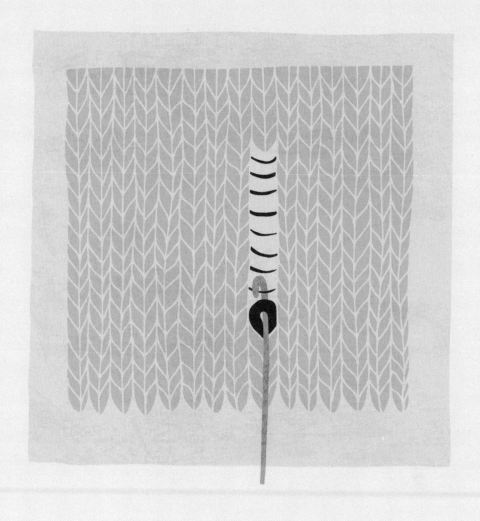

It's quick to mend using this method once you have got the hang of it! The technique is similar to crochet, where you pull the stitches through each other using the crochet hook.

KNITTED PATCH

The aim with this mend is to knit a patch on top of another knitted garment, and it works perfectly for covering damaged areas. If you are an experienced knitter, you can probably make a test swatch to determine what size needles you need to use and which yarn is best suited. Personally, I go with my gut instinct! An advantage with this mend is that it's very quick to unravel if you realize you've done something wrong or decide you want to knit a different pattern.

YOU WILL NEED: *Double-pointed knitting needles. Yarn. Darning needle (if necessary). Iron. Pressing cloth.*

Decide which horizontal stitch row you want the patch to start; it should be a safe distance away from the damaged area. Each stitch is made up of two arms that grip around the stitch above, and it's the left one of this pair of arms that you want to pick up in each stitch (1). Pick up the stitches on a double-pointed knitting needle. Once you've picked up all stitches required, knit one row and then purl one row. When you reach the end of your second row, purl the last stitch together with a new stitch that you pick up from the garment.

To work out which stitch to pick up from the garment, look at those little arm pairs in the stitches: if you pull them apart a little, you'll see there is a horizontal bar running between them. This is what you should pick up. From the first stitch you knitted in the bottom right corner of your work, count one stitch to the right and one stitch up, then pick up the bar going across this stitch by inserting a double-pointed knitting needle to lift the stitch up (2).

So, you've purled the last stitch on your knitting needle together with the new stitch that you just picked up. On the next row, slip the first stitch by simply transferring it over to the right-hand needle. This means that the edge of the patch will become more flexible. When you have finished knitting the next row, you need to pick up the first bar in between the arms on the left-hand side of the work, counting one stitch to the left and two stitches up from the first stitch you knitted in the bottom left corner of the work to find the right stitch. Now you've got the momentum going! Continue to knit and purl alternate rows, slipping the first stitch in each row and knitting/purling the last stitch together with a bar in between the arms (leaving one stitch in between the ones that you pick up) until you have knitted a patch to the required size. When you feel that you're finished, secure the top row of stitches with Swiss darning stitches (see page 95).

If the patch is covering a hole, and not just an area on the garment that's worn thin, it's a good idea to secure the edges of the hole now. I sewed two rows of running stitch around the edge using the same yarn that I used for the patch, and secured the yarn by reverse stitching. I picked up the stitches carefully so that they didn't go through the patch completely; if they had they would have been visible from the outside, which I didn't want!

The only thing left to do now is to secure the threads by sewing a few stitches on the inside of the work and press. Lower the temperature on the iron; a medium heat is good. Use a lot of steam. It's best to leave the work to cool before you put on the garment, as it can stretch while still warm and damp.

1.   2.

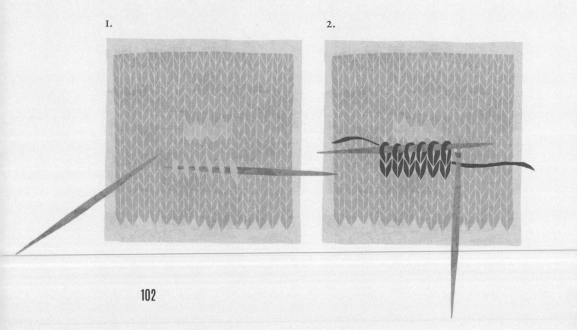

LEATHER CARE

When it comes to repairing leather, contact glue is your best friend. Leather and skin are, unlike textile materials, great for glueing! In most cases you can just glue on a patch, but you can also sew a couple of stitches to keep it in place.

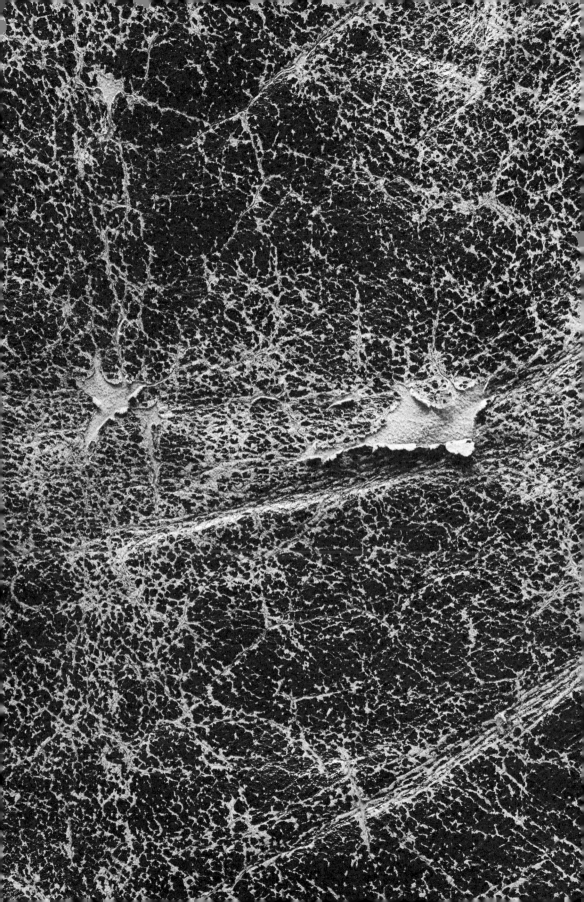

LOOK AFTER YOUR LEATHER GARMENT

There is actually only one thing you need to keep in mind if you want to buy a new leather product, and that is to talk with the person who sells it. If he or she can tell you about the country of origin of the leather, what kind of leather it is and where the product was made, it's a sign that they are engaged and serious. If not, there's a chance you'll get misled and buy something that won't last for that many years! Another question that is good to ask is how the leather has been tanned.

CHROME TANNING is the most common form of tanning and results in durable products that could certainly tear but that, in principle, won't break down in nature at all. In fact, chrome-tanned leather is classed as environmentally hazardous waste and should be handed in to a waste disposal centre instead of being thrown in the bin when the product has been worn out, since it will release a very toxic substance when burnt. The advantage of chrome tanning is that it's cheap!

VEGETABLE TANNING is a lot less common and is not cheap, but it's a more environmentally friendly tanning method. A vegetable-tanned skin is stiffer in the beginning than a chrome-tanned one, but it will soften with time. Sunlight and fat will make these skins darker, and a skin that started its life very light will turn a deep cognac hue after a few years' of wear. A vegetable-tanned leather offers variation, unlike a chrome-tanned leather which won't change that much. Also, veg-tanned skin can, in theory, be composted. Everyone who is now in Team Veg-tan raise a hand!

One main reason for cracks in leather is that the material has dried out, so when you buy a leather product remember that you can extend its lifespan with the right care. A special leather conditioner enables the leather to retain its natural softness, and there are different kinds to choose from. Belts and wallets generally don't need much care, since they get natural fats from being handled, but shoes, jackets and bags may need to be conditioned from time to time.

The best way to determine whether the leather is thirsty is to feel it. If it feels dry, it probably is! I asked a few friends who are shoemakers and they said 'if the leather looks good, it's healthy', and that seems like a good rule of thumb. Start by cleaning the item you're about to treat; you can get special leather soap for this. For cleaning suede, use a damp cloth or the vacuum cleaner. Jackets, bags and softer skins will benefit from a thin layer of conditioner, but when it comes to shoes, my shoemakers recommend just shoe polish: 'Think of caring for your shoes as you would care for your hands: you don't want a layer of sticky cream left on top of them.'

When you are conditioning very dry leather, apply several thin layers of conditioner until it doesn't soak up any more and then wipe off the excess, instead of drowning the leather in fat. It is actually possible to over-grease leather, which can be devastating and lead to it rotting instead.

A garment made out of leather usually has what's called the grain side – the smooth side of the leather – facing outwards. It's the most durable layer and is also the outermost layer of the skin – in other words, the layer that is intended to protect the animal and take the most amount of bashing. The other side is called the flesh side and is usually a bit fuzzier. Sometimes the grain side is sanded down to make a durable but matt surface; this kind of sanded leather is called 'nubuck' or 'split leather'. If you sand down the grain completely from the skin, you get a material that is equally soft and fuzzy on both sides – suede. Nubuck and suede are less durable than leather, which has the outer layer intact, and that's why we usually see the smooth surface on leather products, regardless of whether it's shoes, bags or jackets.

THE DIFFERENCE BETWEEN SKIN AND LEATHER

Both skin and leather are made from tanned animal hides, although the difference between the two isn't always clearly defined. In general, leather is thick and stiff, whereas skin is thin and soft. A tanned hide to which the animal's fur is still attached is usually called a pelt.

MENDING A TEAR IN LEATHER

A tear in leather is best mended from the inside of the garment. With a jacket, you may need to open up the lining in a suitable place to reach the inside behind the tear. Do this before you start glueing to avoid getting stains on the lining! Find a seam close to the hole and open it up carefully using a stitch unpicker. Once you have finished glueing and everything is dry, slipstitch the lining back together again (see page 13).

Since you are mending leather and are using contact glue, the mending patch should also be made out of leather. If the hole is so large that the mending patch will show through it, it's good to try and find leather of the same hue and appearance, but if you only need a patch behind the hole to hold a tear together, I recommend using thin skin or hide. When two pieces of skin or hide are glued together it's best to stick the flesh sides against each other, since they have the best properties for the glue to adhere to. If you want to stick the grain side to the flesh side, rub the grain side a little with a piece of sandpaper to roughen it up, and it will adhere better.

YOU WILL NEED: *Scissors. Leather for a patch. Contact adhesive.*

Cut out a mending patch approximately 1–2 cm (½–¾ in.) larger all around than the tear itself. Brush the adhesive both onto the patch and around the tear. Put the patch in place, press, and then remove the patch again immediately. After approximately 30 seconds, put it in place again and press firmly. The contact adhesive will take well to being worked with like this, meaning that once the patch is in place, the mending will be durable.

Leave the mended garment for a couple of minutes until the adhesive has dried completely and then you can start wearing it again.

It's also possible to stitch around the tear to guarantee that the patch is held in place – but if you do, make sure the adhesive is completely dry, otherwise you'll get glue on your needle.

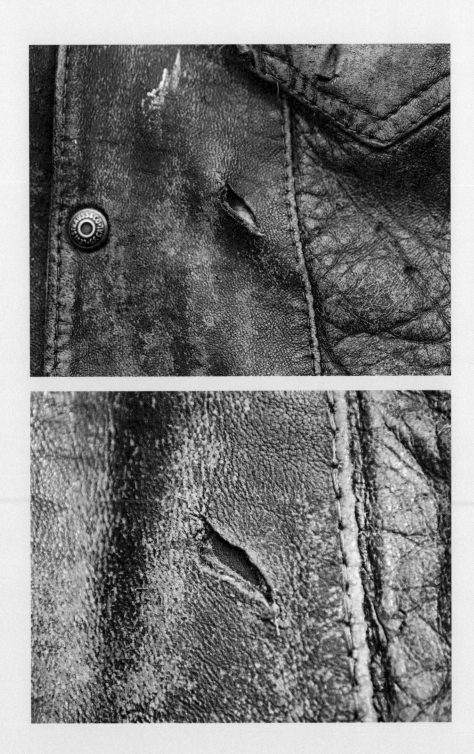

Materials

Let's start at the beginning. All clothes are made from different materials that are woven, knitted or otherwise cobbled together to create a textile. These materials are in turn made from different fibres with different origins and properties. Some come from animals, others from plants and a lot of them are made from plastic. The quality of a garment is fundamentally dependent on what material it is made from, and it can therefore be useful to have some basic knowledge of materials. That way it's easier for you to estimate how long the garment will last, how efficient it will be in keeping you warm and how it will age as you use it and wash it.

Why is wool better suited for some garments? Why do we associate linen with a cooling summer feeling? And not least – why do some garments become wardrobe favourites? You can find the answers to many of these questions by looking at the washing label, which provides information about both the material and its origin. You will get a fairly good pointer from the washing label about whether the garment will be functional over the years to come or if it's a garment that has already passed its best-before date.

Most people have a fairly good idea about what type of materials they prefer to wear and a lot of the sensation sits in the fingertips – so feel the fabric and give it a pinch. Also get into the habit of turning the garment inside out, as this can reveal a lot. The inside can tell you about the working conditions for the person or persons who made the garment. Threads that are hanging loose are a telltale sign that the garment was made by someone with low demand for attention to detail – at a guess, a stressed factory worker.

Watch out for fabrics made from many different fibres, especially a blend of organic and synthetic fibres. The more materials, the higher the risk that the garment will lose its shape after a few washes.

ANIMAL FIBRES

Animal fibres are natural fibres and are also called protein fibres. Among the animal fibres are all types of wool and silk.

WOOL is a collective term for hair from various animals. Wool from merino sheep is the type of fibre that is most common in clothes production today. The merino sheep has been bred to produce a soft, long, crinkled fibre that is well suited to textile production. The sheep are sheared twice a year and afterwards the wool is washed before it's carded and spun into a thread.

Most people probably associate wool with warmth, which is due to the fibre holding a lot of air. And not only that – should a wool garment get wet, it will still keep you warm, since the material can absorb up to 30 per cent of its own weight in water!

Wool fibre also has a dirt-repellent quality, which means that clothes made from wool are easy to care for. To clean them it's usually just enough to brush them off and hang them out to air, since the oxygen in the air helps the wool to clean itself by breaking down dirt particles that then fall off the garment. Sheep's wool contains lanolin, a natural fat that contributes to the wool's warming and self-cleaning properties.

Even though wool is self-cleaning, it will need to be washed sooner or later, and most people are probably aware that a wool garment that is washed the wrong way can shrink into a miniature version of the original. The wool fibre is sensitive to changes in temperature when wet, so hand washing or machine washing on the wool programme is recommended.

If you use a laundry detergent, make sure it's one that's suitable for wool. Avoid washing detergent with enzymes, for example: it's amazing for breaking down proteins in food stains, but it will also break down the wool, which is made of protein.

After washing, wool garments fare best when dried flat, so that they don't get stretched. Lay the garment over a drying rack or on top of a clean, dry towel on the floor and leave it there until dry.

Lint balls will sometimes appear on wool garments, but usually you don't need to worry about them. Continue to wear the garment and they will fall off from wear and tear!

SILK is the name of the fibre that comes from the silkworm. When the larva is ready to pupate, it will spin itself into a cocoon formed of a single long thread. This thread is made from secretions produced in modified salivary glands and forced out of tiny tubes called spinnerets on the larva's mouthparts. There are several different species of silkworm and the most common one is called *Bombyx mori*, also known as the mulberry moth.

In silk production the larva is usually not allowed to reach the moth stage, since the moth would eat its way out of the cocoon and therefore split the thread. The cocoon is instead heated up in hot water or steam that kills the larva, and the thread, which can be up to 300 metres (almost 330 yards) long, is then unwound.

There is also a type of silk called wild silk or ethical silk, where the moth is allowed to leave the cocoon before extracting the thread. The fibre is shorter but can still be spun into a thread.

Silk thread is a light fibre and it has the ability to make you feel warm if you are cold and cool if you are hot. The thread is strong if it's pulled in the direction of the fibre grain; as a fabric it becomes significantly more fragile, and when wet it loses up to 20 per cent of its strength, which is good to keep in mind when washing silk garments. Old silk fabrics can become very fragile when wet, so be careful.

When washing silk the same rule applies as for wool: don't use washing detergents with enzymes, since it will break down the protein in the material and weaken the fibre. You can air out silk garments in between uses, but if they have become sweaty it's good to wash or rinse them, since dried-in sweat makes silk fragile. When washing, hand washing with a mild washing detergent is recommended, and when washing in the machine, a delicate wash at maximum 30°C (86°F) will do the trick. It's a good idea to use a washing bag to protect the garment from damage during the washing process. Also check the washing instructions on the label; if it says dry clean, then follow that recommendation.

Just like wool, silk garments fare best when dried flat. Lay the garment over a drying rack or on the floor on top of a clean, dry towel.

CELLULOSE FIBRES

Cellulose fibres are also natural fibres but they are derived from plants. The most common fibre in textile production is cotton, and it's its relatively low price, combined with its properties, that has made it popular.

COTTON belongs to the genus *Gossypium*, which comprises approximately 50 species of bushes and trees; *Gossypium hirsutum* is the species that is mainly cultivated for textile production. Large cultivations are common in subtropical climates, and cotton is cultivated in many parts of the world, but Egypt, Russia and the USA are the three countries that play a significant role in the world's cotton production.

When the plant's flowers wither, the seed capsules are left, cased in hairy fibres, and it's these fibres that are processed and spun into cotton thread. It's difficult to mention cotton without thinking about the problems associated with it, not least human suffering in the form of the slave trade, which played a significant role in the history of cotton. Today there are also problems with the amount of pesticides used and the fact that cotton is often cultivated in areas prone to droughts, which means that the cultivations are dependent on irrigation.

Cotton fibre gets dirty easily, but since it's also very durable it can take being washed in hot temperatures: 40–60°C (105–140°F) and even up towards 90°C (195°F) is okay, although I think it's unnecessary to always wash in such hot temperatures. Cotton garments are relatively easy to care for, but always remember to read the washing label on the garment to see what's recommended. If the material hasn't been pre-washed, you can expect that the garment will shrink when washed, especially at hotter temperatures. You can stretch out the garment carefully after washing when it's still wet to prevent the shrinkage somewhat. A garment that has been washed once will usually get a few bumps around the seams. The surface of the fabric can become a little fuzzy and the edges can end up with a slightly lighter hue than the rest of the garment.

LINEN comes from the flax plant, *Linum usitatissimum*. Flax is regarded as one of the oldest cultivated plants and has, among other things, been used for the production of yarn, thread and rope. The fibre from this slender-stemmed blue-flowering grass sits in the stem, and to extract the fibre, the plant must go through a four-step process: retting, breaking, scutching and heckling.

Linen has the ability to absorb moisture and most people probably have linen towels at home for this very reason. Just like cotton, linen is a durable material and it's usually no problem to wash linen at 60°C (140°F), but you shouldn't go over 80°C (175°F) since the fibre will then get damaged. Also keep in mind that linen will usually shrink after the first wash, so it's a good idea to ask the seller if the garment or the fabric that you're buying has been pre-washed! Linen fabrics crease but can take being ironed, and if you cold mangle the fabric it will give the linen a particularly nice lustre and feel.

NEVER TUMBLE DRY!

Tumble drying damages all kinds of fabric fibres and will reduce the lifespan of the garment significantly. The fluff in the filter is made out of textile fibres that are much more useful in your garment than in the bin.

HAND WASHING

Fill your sink (or a bucket) with water that is slightly warmer than lukewarm and dissolve a little bit of washing detergent in it. You can buy special hand-wash detergent, but standard washing detergent will do the job fine and in an emergency you can use hand soap or washing-up liquid. Soak the garment and rub a little bit of washing detergent into particularly dirty areas – under the arms, for example. Leave the garment to soak for a bit, around half an hour. Squeeze it a few times while soaking and then rinse it thoroughly by draining the sink, wringing out the garment, filling the sink up with clean water, dipping the garment and squeezing it. Repeat once more with clean water. Wring out the garment and hang up to dry.

I'd like to give a word of caution against squeezing and wringing the garments too hard if they are made from silk or old cotton, since they can become fragile when wet.

WASHING JEANS

First things first: it's a myth that you're not allowed to wash your jeans. The contrast between the worn and unworn areas will indeed become stronger if you refrain from washing your jeans during the first year, but the truth is that jeans that are never washed will wear out quicker than jeans that are washed occasionally! This is because the dirt that gathers will break down the fabric and make it fragile.

If you are worried about getting washing marks on your clothes, try soaking them overnight in cold water before washing them. The fabric will then absorb water and become more flexible, which means it can move around more in the washing machine, thus reducing the risk of marks.

I wash my jeans inside out at 40°C (105°F), but if you feel that's too brutal you can choose a delicate programme instead. They won't spin as much, and instead mostly rock the washing carefully back and forth.

SYNTHETIC MATERIALS

This is a collective term for different kinds of synthetically produced fibres. You can divide them into two categories: synthetic fibres and artificial fibres. Synthetic fibres can be compared to plastics and include polyester, polyamide and acrylic fibres. Artificial fibres, on the other hand, are extracted from nature by regenerating other materials – for example viscose, which is made from cellulose from wood.

Most synthetic materials can be washed at 40°C (105°F), but you should read the washing label to see what's recommended. Remember also that synthetic materials nowadays are often mixed with other materials, so even if a garment feels as if it's made from cotton, it can contain synthetic fibres and should be treated accordingly. As a rule, synthetic fibres are rarely compatible with fabric softener, which can damage the fibre's properties.

Knitted garments made from synthetic materials, especially acrylic, tend to develop a lot of lint balls. Unfortunately, the lint balls won't disappear by themselves, as they would usually do on a garment made purely from wool.

The worst is if the material is a blend of wool and synthetic fibres, which can lead to the wool producing lint balls that then get stuck in the synthetic fibres.

BURN TEST

There is a trick you can use if you're unsure what a garment is made of: pick out a small thread from the inside of the garment and set fire to it! This technique is called the burn test and is best carried out outside or in a well-ventilated room. Set the little thread on fire and observe how it's burning, how it smells once it's burnt out and what the ash looks like, and you can determine what the garment is made of.

WOOL – Will flare up quickly and then burn out. Smells like burnt hair. The ash will get charred and turn into a fine dust.

SILK – Will flare up quickly and then burn out. Smells a little bit like burnt flesh, but not like burnt hair.

COTTON AND VISCOSE – Won't burn out by itself. Smells like burnt paper. The ash is soft and grey.

LINEN – Won't burn out by itself. Smells a bit like burnt grass. The ash is soft and grey.

POLYESTER – Burns for a short while before going out. Forms a hard black bead that smells of melted plastic.

ACRYLIC – Won't burn out by itself. Melts while it burns but won't form a bead in the same way that polyester does.

1.

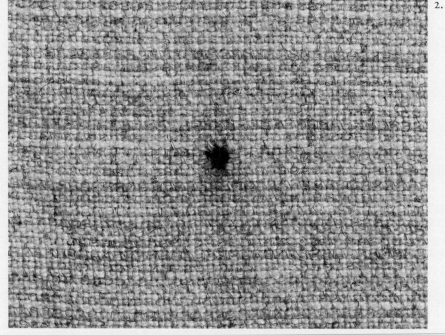

2.

Advanced mending

INVISIBLE MENDING

The aim with invisible mending is to replace damaged fabric in a textile in a way that is as invisible as possible. There are two main branches of invisible mending: either you pick out threads from the fabric from the inside of the garment and weave them in over the damaged area one by one, or you cut out a small piece of fabric from the inside of the garment and attach it over the hole by unpicking the edges of the patch and then weave the threads into the fabric around the hole. It's the latter technique that I present here.

Invisible mending was taught in schools during the '50s and '60s and at that time there were also invisible mending studios where moth-eaten suits, coats and jackets were brought in to be renovated instead of thrown away. It's quite a time-consuming undertaking, so the studios closed down one after the other as textiles became cheaper and people started to buy new clothes instead of handing their old ones in for mending.

This mending technique works by far the best on woven wool fabrics, and as a beginner it's wise to test it out on a coarse fabric with clearly visible threads. It's handy, but not absolutely essential, to have a magnifying glass mounted to the table or on a stand when you work. The construction doesn't really matter; the main thing is to have both of your hands free.

YOU WILL NEED: *Peace and quiet. Good lighting. Table-mounted magnifying glass (optional). Tailor's chalk. Tape measure. Scissors. Fabric for a patch. Needle. Tacking thread. Paper (if necessary). Pins. Blunt needle with large eye. Needle threader (optional). Silk thread or sewing thread in the same colour as the fabric. Iron. Pressing cloth. Darning needle.*

Start by studying the hole in question (2) and decide how large the mending patch should be. The shape of the patch will be square or rectangular and it has to sit at least 5 mm (¼ in.) away from the edge of the hole. Mark the placement of the patch with tailor's chalk, so that you can measure out the length and the width of the patch.

Let's say that the area to be patched measures 3 x 3 cm (1¼ x 1¼ in.). You will need a 6 x 6-cm (2½ x 2½-in.) patch in the same fabric that the garment is made out of, because on each side of the patch you will need an extra 1.5 cm (⅝ in.) of fabric to attach the patch to the fabric around the hole. If you haven't got a patch this size you can, in an emergency, reduce this 'seam allowance' to 1 cm (½ in.) on each side, but no more than that!

If you have a little bit of the fabric that the garment is made out of, you can probably use this for your mending patch, but in most cases you won't and you will have to look inside the garment to see if you can cut out a piece from it. Trousers usually have extra fabric at the legs in case you need to lengthen the trousers, and on jackets there is usually a bottom hem that you can take a little bit from.

Carefully unpick enough lining so that you can reach your intended mending patch easily. If the fabric is patterned – checked, for example – it's super important to find a patch with the exact same pattern in order to make an invisible mending. Once you have got it figured out, mark out your intended patch with tailor's chalk and mark out the side that faces upwards on the fabric. Do the marking on the side of the fabric that faces outwards on the garment, and then you will know which side to face out. Cut out the patch.

Now you've got a garment with a hole on the inside, too. You might just as well mend this straight away, so that you can get on and focus on the invisible mending afterwards! Take a patch from a fabric that is as similar to the garment's fabric as possible, or a patch from a fabric that is as neutral as possible, and sew it over the cut-out area in the same way as you would sew in a patch with folded edges (see page 38). Then sew up the lining with blind hem stitch to put it back in the same place as before you started to unpick it.

Back to our first hole, the one to be invisibly mended!

If the inside of the hole is covered with lining, you will need to make sure not to get it attached to the mending. The easiest way is to slot a piece of paper in between the lining and the outer fabric. The paper will also stiffen the fabric, which can be useful.

3.

4.

5.

6.

Take out your little mending patch and pin it below the hole – place the patch with the chalk marking facing outwards and the up-marking facing upwards, and you will know it's in the right position. It can get very problematic if you place the patch upside down, since the fabric usually catches the light differently depending on what direction you're looking from.

It's now that you need the 'peace and quiet' from the materials list. Start by unpicking the upper edge of the mending patch. Pick out the threads that run horizontally until you have freed 1.5 cm (⅝ in.) of the vertically running threads (1).

Carefully study the fabric on the mending patch and the fabric around the hole you are about to mend. To make it easier, I have chosen to work with a plain-weave fabric, and I'm going to call the threads that run horizontally 'H' and those that run vertically 'V'.

The V-threads that now sit as a fringe on the upper edge of the mending patch had two different starting positions: every other thread ran under an H-thread and every other thread ran over an H-thread.

Move the mending patch up and pin it in place over the hole. You can remove this shortly, but at this stage it's useful to have both hands free! Back to the edge with the V-threads. Start your work 1.5 cm (⅝ in.) in from the left-hand side of the patch. Pick out a couple of V-threads, where the left one has just run over the last H-thread and the one next to it has just run under. Fold these two threads down and secure them temporarily with a pin while you take out your blunt needle.

Now you can start the actual repair! In the left-hand corner of the chalk marking that you made to indicate the size of the mending, pick out a V-thread on the garment that disappears under an H-thread. Insert the blunt needle exactly at the point where the V-thread disappears under the H-thread and then, without pulling the needle through, bring it out approximately 1 cm (½ in.) away. Leave the needle inserted in the fabric in this position at the same time as you edge it in between the gap formed in the fringe of the mending patch from the two threads that you secured with a pin. Remove the pin that keeps these two threads in place and insert the threads into the eye of the needle (3). If you find this tricky, use a needle threader.

Now pull the needle through the thread! The two threads that you inserted into the needle's eye will now follow the needle through the fabric and, when the needle has come out on the other side, they will run through the needle's eye so that they protrude from the fabric 1 cm (½ in.) away from the edge of the mending patch. Thereafter you pick out two new threads to the right of the ones you just sewed in, insert the needle into the place where the next V-thread disappears in under the same H-thread that you just went under, insert the two threads into the needle's eye and pull through.

Continue doing this until you are 1.5 cm (⅝ in.) away from the right-hand edge of the mending patch. Then turn the work 90 degrees so that the right-hand edge faces upwards. Now you have to release more threads so that you can sew in this edge as well. To do this, unpick the H-threads along the edge until you reach the last H-thread that you inserted into the garment (4). Be careful as you approach, so that you don't unpick too many!

Now comes a tricky step – getting the beginning of the new row into a good position in relation to the last one. What you have to do is to take a deep breath, look carefully and try to think logically. On a plain-woven fabric you can usually figure out where to start the new row with a bit of brain power!

When you have managed to get past the corner, work your way to the next corner, then repeat until you get to the third one. Once all four edges are woven in, you can congratulate yourself on a job well done! Sometimes the last corner won't match up, and you can choose when you get there whether you want to unpick and redo the mending or not. Some fabrics will only give you one chance, since the threads can start to become loose as you thread them through the fabric around the hole. In that case you will have to be content with the fact that you at least haven't got a large hole anymore!

Now you need to secure the mending patch in place. For this you need a thread that is as thin as possible and the best trick is to take a silk thread and divide it in three: that is, untwist the strands that the thread is built up from and pull out one of them. Discard this one, pick up what remains (a thin thread made from two strands) and thread the needle with this. Secure with a small knot on the inside of the work and sew with tiny pick stitches in a narrow zigzag that runs through the mending patch and the surrounding fabric. Place this 'seam' about two threads away from the groove that appears at the joint. Don't pull the pick stitches too tight, otherwise the thread will become taut on the reverse of the joint and push it upwards. Usually this won't become apparent until you press – and then it will be too late to do anything about it because the stitches are so tiny that this seam is incredibly difficult to unpick. So pull the thread, but don't pull it too tight (5).

When you have worked your way around the whole patch, secure the thread by sewing past the point where you started. Then cut off the thread close to the surface of the fabric so that the end disappears into the fabric.

Now it's time for the first of two rounds of pressing. Press with a damp pressing cloth over a soft base – a padded ironing board, for example. Then pull all the thread ends that protrude on the front of the garment to the back. The easiest way to do this is to work from the reverse of the repair. Take your darning needle and carefully pull the threads, and they will slip through easily. If you can't reach to pull them out from the back, insert the darning needle from the front and carefully coax the threads through to the back (6). Press again, this time on a firmer base (a chopping board covered with a tea towel usually works well). The cloth should now be slightly damp – not wet, but not bone dry either. Once you are happy with your pressing, you are done!

When the mending is finished, it is virtually invisible!

THANKS TO
Douglas – without you, no book!
Hampus Andersson for photo sessions during the hottest summer ever.
Terése Karlsson and Sebastian Wadsted for beautiful design and illustrations.
Elisabeth Fock and Maria for encouragement and coaching.
Emelie and Dennis for leather expertise.
Karin and Gunn for craft expertise.

FIRST PUBLISHED IN THE UNITED KINGDOM IN 2019 BY
PAVILION
43 GREAT ORMOND STREET
LONDON WC1N 3HZ

COPYRIGHT © PAVILION BOOKS COMPANY LTD 2019
© 2018 KERSTIN NEUMÜLLER
ORIGINAL TITLE: LAPPAT & LAGAT
FIRST PUBLISHED BY NATUR & KULTUR, SWEDEN
PHOTOGRAPHY: HAMPUS ANDERSSON
GRAPHIC DESIGN: SEBASTIAN WADSTED
ILLUSTRATION: TERÉSE KARLSSON

ISBN 978-1-91162-493-6

A CIP CATALOGUE RECORD FOR THIS BOOK IS AVAILABLE FROM THE
BRITISH LIBRARY.

10 9 8 7 6 5 4 3 2

PRINTED AND BOUND BY 1010 PRINTING INTERNATIONAL LTD, CHINA

WWW.PAVILIONBOOKS.COM